ACC

MW01146163

AND

COMMITMENT

THERAPY

RECLAIM YOUR LIFE, REDUCE THE STRESS AND MANAGE YOUR THOUGHTS WITH THE BEST STRATEGIES (ACT PREP GUIDE)

BY

Alexander Harris

Table of content

9

14

COPYRIGHT

This book:

"Acceptance and Commitment Therapy: Realm your life, reduces the stress, and manages your thoughts with the best strategies (Act prep guide)."

Written By

Alexander Harris

This document aims to provide precise and reliable details on this subject and the problem under discussion.

A legal or qualified guide is required. A person must have the right to participate in the field.

A statement of principle is a subcommittee of the American Bar Association, a committee of publishers, and is approved. A copy, reproduction, or distribution of parts of this text, in electronic or written form, is not permitted.

The recording of this document is strictly prohibited. Any retention of this text is only with the written permission of the publisher and all liberties authorized.

The information provided here is correct and reliable, as any lack of attention or other means resulting from the misuse or use of the procedures or instructions contained therein is the total and absolute obligation of the user addressed.

INTRODUCTION

Communication is a tool that we use every day to communicate messages and understand the meaning. Communication is the sharing of knowledge between two or more individuals. This kind of contact uses techniques such as communicating, hearing, writing, and reading. Signs, drawing, dancing, and storytelling, however, are also ways of communicating. In addition, thoughts are communicated to others not only through spoken or written sentences but also through sign or body language. In comparison to casual conversations, therapeutic communication is a purposeful method of communication used in helping relationships. It is an interpersonal relationship between the psychologist and the patient during which the patient's special need is specialists facilitates an efficient exchange of information. The aim of healing dialogue is to provide a safe space for the patient to look at the nature of understanding of the condition and to provide the knowledge and emotional support that each person requires in order to reach the best degree of health and well-being. Therapeutic communication is also separate from that of social communication. This book explores the idea of therapeutic contact and its significance in the treatment of clients, using insights from my most recent experience as a licensed counselor. The benefits of using therapeutic contact in my career and to the client will be outlined. It also involves communication theory as a paradigm and its processes in the use of therapeutic communication and in the use of communication strategies to communicate efficiently. Acceptance and Commitment Therapy (ACT) is a framework therapy that has originated from the cognitive-behavioral psychotherapy family. ACT offers a trans-theoretical paradigm that encompasses perceptual, physiological existential, and communitarian elements; its composition speaks to professionals from a range of contexts. ACT provides an additional set of treatment targets that appears to be more workable. ACT maintains that our greatest human asset, our capacity to construct and use words, is also a director of psychology since it is through stories that we re-experience traumatic histories and become caught in unhealthful pursuits. The problem starts when ideas become rigidly controlling actions, independent of contradictory experimental input. For example, people may ignore obstacles because they believe their thoughts (i.e., 'I can't do it because I'm incompetent').

CHAPTER 1: INTRODUCTION TO ACCEPTANCE AND COMMITMENT

What is the mind?

Does your brain ever say something like this to you? I do it. And so, makes the mind of every psychiatrist I've ever heard about it. Now take a minute to think about what else your mind is doing. It's not helpful. For instance, does it ever compare you to others or judge your efforts, or convince you that you can't do anything you want to do? Is it still pulling the negative thoughts of the past? Do you find fault with your life as it is now and conjure up alternate experiences that will make you so much happier? Can it ever pull you into terrifying situations of the future and alert you about the possible problems that could go wrong? If so, it seems like you've got a typical human mind. You see, in ACT, we start with the premise that normal psychological functions in an ordinary human mind are readily harmful. Sooner or later, they generate psychological misery for all of us. And ACT speculates that human language itself is the source of this distress.

Mind and the language

Human language is a highly complex system of representations, including words, images, tones, facial expressions, and body gestures. Humans use language in two areas: public and private. General use of language involves reading, speaking, whistling, gesturing, drawing, painting, carving, singing, performing, and acting so on. Private use of language involves thought, creativity, daydreaming, organizing, visualizing, contemplating, wondering, and having fantasies, and so on. (A term widely used for private usage of language is cognition). Now, the mind is not a "thing" or "stuff." We use the term "mind" to define an extraordinarily complicated collection of interactive cognitive processes, such as assessing, comparing, reviewing, preparing, recalling, visualizing, etc. And all these dynamic systems depend on the intricate set of symbols that we call human language. Thus, when we use the term "mind" in ACT, we use it as a symbol for "human language."

Your mind is not your partner or your opponent.

ACT sees the imagination as a double-edged sword. It's beneficial for all kinds of reasons, but if we don't understand how to do it efficiently, it's going to hurt us. On the bright side, language lets us make maps and models of the world; anticipate and plan for the future; exchange knowledge; learn from the past; envision things that have never happened and continue to build them. It establishes laws that direct our actions efficiently and allow us to succeed as a community, connect with others who are far away, and learn from others who are no longer alive. The negative side of language is that we use it to deceive, exploit, and deliberately mislead; to spread accusation, libel, and ignorance; to provoke anger, hatred, and violence. It also uses to make weapons of mass destruction and mass pollution industries; to reflect on and "relive" the painful events of the past; to intimidate ourselves by predicting negative futures. To equate, judge, denounce, and condemn both ourselves and others; since language is both a gift and a curse, we always say in ACT, "Your mind isn't your friend — and it isn't your enemy either." So now that we know what "mind" is, let's turn to a fascinating issue.

What is the purpose of the ACT?

The purpose of ACT, in broad terms, is to build a prosperous, complete, and fruitful life while embracing the pain that eventually comes with it. Later in this segment, we will look at a more technical concept of ACT, but first take a moment to answer this question:

why does life eventually entail pain? There are many explanations for this. We will also feel anger, dissatisfaction, rejection, defeat, and failure. We're all going to experience sickness, disability, and maturity. We will always face our mortality and the loss of our loved ones.

On top of that, certain simple human emotions, natural feelings that every one of us will regularly encounter in our lives are inherently painful: terror, sorrow, regret, rage, shock, and disgust, to name but a few. And as if all that wasn't enough, each of us has a mind that can conjure up misery at any time. Thanks to human language, everywhere we go, whatever we do, we will feel pain right away. At every time, we can relive a traumatic memory or lose ourselves in an ominous prediction of the future. Or we might get wrapped up in unfavorable similarities ("Her work is easier than mine") or pessimistic self-esteem ("I'm too fat," "I'm not clever enough," and so on). Thanks to human language, even on the best days of our lives, we might feel pain. For example, suppose it's Susan's wedding day, and all her friends and family are gathered together to rejoice in her happy new relationship. She's pleased. But then she's saying that I wish my dad were here, and she recalls how he committed suicide when she was just 16 years old. Now, one of the best days of her life, she's in agony.

And all of us are in the same boat as Susan. What we need to do is consider a moment when something terrible has happened or envision a future when something terrible is happening. Or judge ourselves unfairly, or equate our life to someone else that seems more substantial, and we are suffering immediately. Thus, due to the sophistication of the intellect, even the most fortunate human life invariably entails considerable suffering. Unfortunately, ordinary human beings typically deal with their grief ineffectively. Many, as we encounter unpleasant emotions, feelings, and sensations, we react in ways that are self-defeating or self-destructive in the long run. Because of this, one of the main aspects of ACT is to educate people on how to treat pain more efficiently with the use of cognitive therapy.

What is mindfulness?

"Mindfulness" is an old term used in a broad range of ancient religious and philosophical practices, including Buddhism, Taoism, Hinduism, Judaism, Islam, and Christianity. Western psychology has only recently begun to consider the many advantages of learning mindfulness abilities. If you read a few books on mindfulness, you will find that "mindfulness" is described in a lot of ways, but they are interpreted differently. It comes down to this: mindfulness requires paying attention to versatility, transparency, and curiosity. This basic description shows us three important things to do. First, concentration is a method of consciousness, not a process of thought. It means raising consciousness or paying attention to your experience at this time, rather than getting "caught up" in your feelings. Secondly, mindfulness requires a particular attitude: one of openness and curiosity. And if the encounter at this moment is complicated, painful, or upsetting, you should be open to it and curious about it instead of running away or struggling with it. Third, mindfulness requires versatility in your concentration: the capacity to intentionally direct, extend, or focus your attention on various aspects of your experience.

We should use mindfulness to "wake up," to communicate with ourselves, and to understand the fullness of the moment of life. We will use it to develop our self-knowledge and understand more about how we feel, perceive, and respond. We will use it to create a meaningful and personal bond with the people we care for, including ourselves. So, we will use it to actively affect our actions, so expand our spectrum of reactions to the environment in which we work. Consciously, the art of living is a profound approach to improve psychological strength and improve life satisfaction. There's a lot more to ACT than just mindfulness, of course. It is also about appreciated living: taking action, continuously, that is directed and consistent with core values. Indeed, in ACT, we teach mindfulness skills for the express intention of promoting cherished activity: to help people live by their values. In other words, the objective that we strive to accomplish in the ACT is conscious, positive life. This will become evident in the next segment, where we look at the six main ACT processes.

Acceptance and Commitment Therapy (ACT)

Acceptance and Commitment Therapy (ACT) is a framework therapy that has originated from the cognitive-behavioral psychotherapy family. ACT offers a trans-theoretical paradigm that encompasses perceptual, physiological, existential, and communitarian elements; its composition speaks to professionals from a range of contexts. ACT provides an additional set of treatment targets that appears to be more workable. ACT maintains that our greatest human asset, our capacity to construct and use words, is also a director of psychology since it is through stories that we re-experience traumatic histories and become caught in unhealthy pursuits. The problem starts when ideas become rigidly controlling actions, independent of contradictory experimental input. For example, people may ignore obstacles because they believe their thoughts (i.e., 'I can't do it because I'm incompetent'). In a western society that encourages reason-giving ('Why can't you do it?'), people get addicted to self-description and find it hard to behave differently. The method of interpreting thoughts as fact, rather than the on-going process of thinking, is associated with cognitive fusion and is assumed to trap people in persistent behavioral patterns. ACT acknowledges that our social dialogue idealizes optimistic feelings. A glance at every magazine will show hundreds of 'quick fix' ideas that are sure to deliver pleasure.

And more daunting feelings are ever-present in a world afflicted by natural disasters, incidents, violence, financial and emotional instability. These negative emotions are also perceived as 'evil' and are followed by attempts to prevent or discourage them.

ACT uses the word 'experiential prevention' to describe people's efforts to monitor unwanted internal perceptions. Interestingly, efforts to suppress internal discomfort incidents can simply amplify them, whereas other prevention methods (e.g., alcohol, substance usage, procrastination) can have unhelpful long-term implications. Indeed, the study indicates that experiential prevention is associated with an elevated risk of psychopathology. In the ACT paradigm, experimental prevention and cognitive convergence are two key processes that underpin psychological rigidity, marked by a deep commitment to one's intellect and resulting behavioral inflexibility. For instance, a person may avoid expressing moments of weakness with his or her partner to block feelings of insecurity, while they may be of benefit to a relation of connectedness. Acceptance and Commitment Therapy (ACT) helps participants to embrace their emotions and opinions rather than fight or feel wrong about them. It may sound overwhelming at first, but ACT, combined with mindfulness-based therapy, provides clinically successful care. Health disorders such as anxiety, depression, OCD, alcohol, and drug misuse will all benefit from ACT and Mindfulness-Based Cognitive Therapy (MBCT). ACT develops relational resilience and is a type of behavioral therapy that incorporates mindfulness skills with self-acceptance.

Commitment plays a vital part when it comes to further recognition of your emotions and feelings. In the case of ACT, you commit to facing the issue head-on instead of escaping tension. Imagine dedicating yourself to acts that will lead to making your experience smoother and to take on any task.

As you can see later in this chapter, the ACT is useful for a wide variety of psychiatric problems. It is also helpful as a life-affirming and inspirational view of self-determination. What if you could recognize and encourage yourself to believe what you're feeling, even if it's negative?

Core therapeutic processes of acceptance and commitment therapy

Six main ACT mechanisms direct patients through treatment and offer a basis for improving therapeutic flexibility. These six main ACT processes consist of the following components:

- Acceptance
- Diffusion of cognition
- To be present
- Self-context
- Values
- A dedication to action

Acceptance is an antidote to our tendency to stop worrying about a negative or theoretically harmful experience. It is an active decision to encourage adverse events to occur without seeking to reject or alter them. Acceptance is not the objective of the ACT, but a way of promoting intervention that can lead to positive outcomes.

Cognitive diffusion refers to strategies designed to alter the way a person responds to his or her thoughts and feelings. Acceptance and Dedication Therapy is not meant to minimize our response to traumatic experiences, but rather to face them and to leave the other side with a diminished fixation on these experiences. Being present may be understood as the process of being mindful of the present moment, without the judgment of experience. In other words, it means experiencing what's going on without attempting to anticipate or alter the experience. Self as the context is the notion that a person is not merely the sum of his or her perceptions, feelings, or emotions. The process of "self as a sense" provides the alternate definition that there is a self-independent of present experience. We're not just what happens to us. We are the people that are seeing what happens to ourselves. Values, in this sense, are the qualities that we want to aspire for at any given moment. We all hold values, whether consciously or unconsciously, that lead our steps. In the ACT, we use resources that help us live our lives in line with the ideals we hold dear. Finally, ACT seeks to make patients stick to behaviors that will make them to accomplish their long-term aspirations and to live a life compatible with their beliefs. Positive behavioral changes cannot occur without the knowledge of how this behavior impacts us. ACT is not all that distinct from most behavioral-based therapies; it merely stresses acceptance rather than prevention, which therefore varies from many other types of treatment.

The Function of ACT in behavior and mindfulness

Acceptance and Commitment Counseling is based on Relational Frame Philosophy, a philosophy based on the premise that our desire to communicate is the basis of language and comprehension. Relating means noting the aspects in which the interaction occurs. For instance, we can associate an apple with an orange. Still, our ability to connect helps us to realize that while they have a similar form (round) and purpose (to be eaten), they have different colors and textures. Humans, unlike most other species, have an extraordinary capacity to relate neutral events, as well as unrelated words and concepts. While this is a beneficial skill, it also encourages negative thinking and judgment about oneself. If we can apply the term "cookie" to the experience of eating a cookie, so we can also use the name "worthless" to the sense that we are meaningless. Our ability to construct social networks (e.g., I apply the words "orange," "an apple," and "pear" to the definition of "fruit") can be harmful when anxiety and depression affect us. For example, we might equate "less value" to the opportunity to do my job and, by implication, the term "less value" to my life. ACT is based on Relational Frame Theory. We also form social networks that are not complimentary or life-giving. Still, we can also change such interactions as we practice mindfulness to recognize our emotions and change how we respond and adapt to them, instead of attempting to escape them.

ACT's psychopathology paradigm

The purpose of ACT is to improve psychological health – the capacity to live life as a whole, in contact with the present moment – and to adjust actions based on real-life experience and long-term principles. Psychological resilience is associated with a reduced risk of experiencing a psychiatric illness and is cultivated by six intertwined mechanisms.

Six acceptance and commitment therapy concepts

The principle of Recognition and Dedication Counseling is six fundamental concepts. They work closely for the key objectives of successfully managing traumatic thoughts and memories and developing a rich, vital life. The principles are as follows:

- Behavioral diffusion
- Extension and recognition
- Contact and relation to the present moment
- The Self Observing

- Clarification of concepts
- Action was taken

Now, let's take a quick look at what they require.

1. Behavioral diffusion

This ability is about to learn and interpret emotions, pictures, memories, and other behavioral patterns. For what they are – little more than parts of language and images, rather than what they sometimes seem to be: dangerous events, laws that must be observed, or factual realities and evidence. The opposite neurological process — cognitive fusion — refers to the blending of cognitions (products of the mind, such as feelings, images, or memories) with the objects they relate. In cognitive fusion, for example, our mind can have the same response to the word "chocolate cake" as if

47

we were faced with a slice of it. That is the sheer presence of the stimuli – the words "chocolate cake" – may be enough to launch us drooling, remembering the delicious taste and feeling the thick, fluffy texture of the frosting in our mouths. In a state of cognitive fusion, it appears as if:

- Offense Feelings are a reality: as if what we think is happening.
- Faithful Thoughts are the truth: we believe them.
- Thoughts are essential: we take them seriously, give them our full attention.
- Ideas are orders: we follow them unconsciously.
- Views are wise: we believe they know best, and we take their counsel.
- Feelings are threats: let them frighten or annoy us.

Although, as any dietitian will warn you, the word or picture of a chocolate cake is not the same (at least in terms of both enjoyment and caloric intake!) as the real deal. The cognitive diffusion process aims to isolate negative, unwelcome thoughts, desires, impulses, memories, or other items of the mind from ourselves. It's a step back from them (a method called misidentification in rituals such as psych synthesis) to get a viewpoint and see what they are: just a piece of language going by. The useful application of cognitive diffusion contributes to a more spacious psyche, as we see by the second concept.

2. Extension and recognition

Named "acceptance" by some other ACT professionals and scholars, this ability is called "expansion" because "acceptance" is filled with different definitions. It refers to the process of making room for uncomfortable thoughts, sensations, and desires instead of attempting to avoid or drive them out. Through opening up and encouraging them to come and go without dealing with them, running away from them, or giving them unnecessary publicity, we find that they annoy us a lot less. They're also going quicker, instead of sticking about and annoying us. Imagine the case with a customer who says, "I'm too nervous about going out on a date. I'm so scared that I'm not going to have something to tell or that I'm going to say anything very stupid. "By using CBT methods, we, as psychologists, might help the client dispute the pessimistic perception that she's a bad conversationalist or a dull date. She is replacing her insecure feelings with optimistic, assertive ones, such as being fascinating, excellent at talking, or a worthy social partner.

Through longer psychotherapeutic cycles, we will help her uncover the experiences of her history (probably early childhood) that have made her feel socially awkward. Psychotherapy, though, takes a long time because even though the effect of prior trauma on current practice is understood. There is also a "battle of words" as the various voices within its – the supportive and the assertive – demand for recognition. Being in a battle of this kind is a significant drain on resources. The ACT theory of expansion/acceptance acts differently. It would ask the patient to assume that she's going to go out for a date. She would then be told to scan her body, observing that she had the most extreme fear. Let's say that she said she'd got a big lump in her throat. Then she would be asked to study the lump feeling as if she were a scientist who had never seen anything like it before: to note the shape, weight, vibration, temperature, pulsation, and other dimensions of it. She'd be asked to breathe into the lump, to make room for it, to encourage it to be there (even though we'd be very empathetic in knowing that she didn't want it or want it there!). She could be given the "homework" between sessions to practice observing her lump of fear: not attempting to get rid of it, but only letting the lump feel, and probably other feelings associated with anxiety, come and go as they please: noticing them, not suppressing them, but also not engaging them.

3. Contact and relation to the present moment

To encourage ourselves to perceive the sensations, emotions, and thoughts that have arisen is to obey the third concept of ACT, that of having contact with the present moment "communication." It means living in the moment, reflecting on everything we do, and taking complete knowledge to the here-and-now experience: with transparency, curiosity, and receptivity, instead of focusing on the past or thinking about the future. We are profoundly connected to what's going on right here, right now. With association, we are entirely involved with everything we do. In exercising the relation, we might ask: why bother to take ourselves out of the past or the future to get back to the present moment? Why is this thought to be so helpful to us? Harris points out three main explanations for this:

This is the only life we have (even for those who believe in things such as reincarnation, this is the only life we are aware of right now or seem to know about), so why not make the best of it? It's a half-present to miss half of it. Lack of present-time interaction is akin to listening to a beloved piece of music with earbuds in the ears or enjoying a favorite snack while the mouth is already numb from a visit to the dentist; we lack the richness that should be there. It's the only time we have some control right now. Provided that the ACT Foundation is dedicated to appropriate, value-driven action, we should remind clients that to build a productive life, the story is required, and the capacity to act resides only in the present moment. As the Arab saying goes, "You cannot raise a camel that has not yet arrived (the future), or that has already left (the past)." "Taking action" requires successful action and not just some older activity. Effective action in the ACT is described as that which helps us step in a valued direction. To figure out how the path lies, we need to be mentally present to be aware of what is going on, how we are responding, and then how it is right for us to respond. Harris recommends remembering the mnemonic for the ACT: "Consider your inner experience and be present; pick a cherished direction; and take action": ACT.

And those who appear to live their lives by the mediating power of their emotions usually have some experience of the present-moment-contact: moments when it occurs suddenly and abruptly. The client fearing social ineptness, for example, might be asked to focus on at any moment when she may have been utterly engrossed in being with someone else (date or otherwise): the memory of, say, hanging on every phrase the person spoke, noting the gestures made by their mouth as they told, remembering the person's smell, and how their hair was combed (or not). Complete interaction with another human is likely to have ejected (but temporarily) feelings of social inadequacy from her mind. It is not necessary to exercise this ability on an actual date (in the case of a person who fears social ineptitude) or to have another person around. In the current moment, we can ground ourselves wherever or however we want, only by tuning in. For example, an ACT therapist might encourage a person to consider any small part of their experience of taking a shower. The sensation of the water as it reaches the skin and runs down. The sight of rising steam in the bathroom, or the fragrance of any soaps or other items applied to the body during the shower or after-shower treatment process. Or a person might exercise the present-moment-connection theory by witnessing the minute specifics of the dishwashing experience after dinner: the clinking sound of the plates at the top of the bench, the feeling of the soapy water washing over them, the sight and sound of squeaking as the things made me completely clean, and the visual experience of putting them on the drainboard.

Even easier: an ACT-oriented psychologist might send the client a single piece of food, say, a dried fig, and encourage the person to concentrate on nothing except enjoying it. The client must be advised that intrusive thoughts and emotions must arise; they may be prompted to come and go as they please; the client's mind should stay concentrated on the fruit. However, the communication/contact with the current moment happens; it happens by the Observing Self.

4. The self-observing

Self-Observing is a powerful component of human consciousness, often overlooked by Western psychology. Connecting with its connectivity to a transcendent sense of self:

a consistency of consciousness that is unchanging, ever-present, and impossible to hurt from this most holistic view of oneself. It is possible to perceive explicitly the claims found in certain body-feelings-mind relaxations that, "I am my body, and I am more than my body; I am more than my feelings, and I am more than my feelings; I am more than my mind, and still I am more than my mind." From this position, we can experience that our emotions, perceptions, memories, urges, sensations, images, places, and physical bodies are secondary aspects of ourselves. Still, while they are continually evolving, they are not the core of who we are. To understand the concept of the Observing Self is to realize that as we become conscious of our emotions, there are two mechanisms taking place: that of thinking and that of observing reflection. We should draw the client's attention – again and again, if necessary – to the difference between the feelings that occur and the self that experiences them. From the viewpoint of the Witnessing Self, no internal perception (i.e., thinking, emotion, image, or urge) is harmful or restricting.

We said earlier that the six values work together to help us build a meaningful life. We should now say that the present-moment relation is occurring to the Observing Self. The Observing Self is claimed to be non-judgmental by nature since assumptions are perception, and thus the result of the thinking self. The Witnessing Self does not deal with reality; it sees things as they are without fighting them. It is only when we judge things — such as "evil," "unfair," or "mean"—that we avoid them. It's, then, the dreaming self that informs us that "life shouldn't be the way it (reality) is," that we'd be better if we were somewhere else, someone else, or somehow different. It is also our thought self that places a shield of delusion between ourselves and life, disconnecting us from reality by boredom, diversion, or opposition. The Witnessing Self, on the other hand, is unaware of boredom or resistance. It welcomes every sensation, every encounter, with openness, curiosity, and interest. The Observing Self, still present and accessible, can transcend this, to awaken us, and to bind us to the limitless possibilities of human experience that we may meet, regardless of whether the experience is novel or familiar. Paradoxically, when engaging the Investigating Self when we observe negative encounters, we frequently find that the things we dreaded are much less troubling than they were before. Items are being viewed differently.

Connecting with the Observing Self is a ready capacity to misidentify from suffering and unhappiness. When we stand in the shoes of the (misidentified) Examining Self, we may still experience pain and sadness (our thinking selves may even send us thoughts that we hurt or are unhappy). Always, not all of our consciousness is mixed up with that because some of it includes the Examining Selves in seeing us feel pain. Thus, reality becomes more bearable as we experience, by the option of two places in which to be, a more expansive subconscious. In the context of any particular experience, we may select – either knowingly or unconsciously, by necessity – where we stand. Our decision is dictated by the principles that we possess, so the main component of successful living is to be consistent about what those principles are.

5. Clarification of concepts

This ACT theory is about clarifying what is most necessary for us to have access to in the deepest part of ourselves. It includes wondering what kind of person we want to be, what is important to us, and what we want to stand for in this life. Our principles give direction to our lives and inspire us to make significant improvements. Driven by ideals, not only can we feel a more profound sense of mission and pleasure, but we also see that life can be rich and rewarding even when "wrong" things happen to us. Thus, ACT-oriented therapy may ask the participant to complete a "life values" questionnaire, which asks respondents to focus on their values in ten areas, from family and marital relationships through education and faith to community life and relationship with the natural world. Some clients may like to miss the value clarification tasks, and there might be many explanations why this is so. Many citizens may not be sure about the distinction between beliefs and priorities. The researcher states that ambitions are a one-shot transaction where ideals are so, although they are consistent with our life as things, we consider essential. He uses the example of someone who's moving on a trip, meaning he's going to keep traveling west. The exact direction is equivalent to a value since no matter how far a person may go, there is still a more western direction in which to continue. It is a goal, though, to claim that he wants to ascend to the peak of a specific mountain along the way, so if he climbs to the top of the hill, he has accomplished the goal, and it is a deal. When we know what we believe, we will set concrete targets to abide by our values. But there could be another hindrance to the enactment of this theory.

But are they my actual values? Some persons can oppose the enactment of Principle 5 or even the completion of any questionnaires because they are unsure if the answers they provide represent their "true" beliefs. Of course, just because someone thinks they value something — say, being compassionate — it can be counted as their value because, by definition, value is something we hold dear. Only to respond that we value a thing over anything is to cherish it, to have it as a value. This is a related objection to the one who claims that I don't know what I want. Again, whatever we can pick is our value, purely because we've valued it by calling it. Yet it begs the dilemma of what if my beliefs are in contrast with each other? It is believed that if you are trying to support clients using ACT methodologies, you will find this one; it is true. It is difficult to impossible not to have values that pull one in various directions, particularly in hectic modern life. For example, a client will value early the importance of quality time with the family and, almost as dearly, desire to rise through the ranks at work while paying immediate attention to it; both priorities are likely to clash at some point, if not daily. The truth is that often we have to choose one realm above another, asking ourselves, "What's more important in my life at this moment, considering the contradictory values I'm experiencing?" The person must then function on the value selected, without caring about what he or she is missing from, understanding that, if necessary, and the balance can be" corrected "at a later point. Even others object to clarifying their principles based on historical disappointment or anger.

I don't want to hear about it; I'm just setting myself up to be upset. Many who have endured a lot of anger or inability to live chosen ideals may be afraid to accept what they truly desire, for fear that – again – they may struggle to do so. These twin objections to preferring simple principles talk of "I can't change," "I'm only going to lose," or "I don't deserve any better" doubts that exist throughout several souls. The past is the past, and it cannot be changed, but the future is beginning right now. Clients expressing this kind of frustration should be helped to relax into their agitation and understanding that these comments are just thoughts; they should come and go while the client refocuses on the assessment exercise. I'm going to do that today. Oh, okay. As a psychologist or other mental health assistant, you're likely to have heard this one before! Principle 5 of the meaning clarification can go nowhere while the procrastination beast is roaming. Say the client that it's "later" now, and time to do what's in the very name of ACT counseling.

6. Action was taken

In this last theory, the individual sets goals and takes action: but not just any story. Here the person recognizes that the rich and meaningful life he/she seeks is generated by taking constructive action that is driven by the values he/she prefers. Do adherents have a flawless record of achieving the targets they set themselves? No, of course not, but no matter how many times anyone can "go off the rails." Or even get off the road – the principles are there to encourage and drive the effort to be done again. The aims are there to remind the participant of the actions that would allow him or her to arrive at a visualized existence. In the final analysis, it is up to each person to deliver the will and the energy to take action. We may see an analogy in a future traveler who just needs to go to Africa. The person buys informative, and tour guide books on Africa, contacts travel agencies, and schedules travel plans for the unique locations he wants to visit. He's sure his life is going to be perfect if he can just get to Africa! He's not going to be around on all of his scheduled tours. Because nothing can change in his life at all – until he gets out of the chair, packs his luggage, and comes up on the designated day to board the aircraft. No amount of reading about Africa is going to give him the real impression of Africa that he needs. It must supply the will and resources to go there to transform the rich and positive experience of Africa.

Acceptance and Commitment Counseling (ACT) is a "third-wave" cognitive-behavioral technique intended to improve our interpersonal flexibility. Rather than ignoring or preventing psychological experiences, the ACT is based on the assumption that recognition and mindfulness are more adaptive approaches to the inevitability of existence. By experiencing our thoughts, physical feelings, and emotions in more fluid forms, the acceptance dedication therapists claim, we will reduce the harmful attitudes that they sometimes contribute to it. As an action, ACT has a theoretical basis and has been a reasonably well-established feature of applied positive psychology in recent decades.

Acceptance and expansion worksheets

1) Don't worry about your thinking worksheet

Suppression and prevention have adverse consequences over time. As ill-adapted tactics, they also seem to work against us rather than to our advantage — enhancing the social experience we're trying to avoid. By creating this 'rebound' effect, this acceptance exercise helps therapists to help clients understand this. This workbook has two pieces in it. First, though, it helps to clarify the role of mindfulness in dealing with intrusive emotions, feelings, and memories. The client is then advised to:

- Have them quantify and write down how many they have crossed their minds during the week.
- Then, for several minutes, invite them to try to suppress undesirable feelings, whatever they might want to

do. The third suggestion on this worksheet asks them to estimate how much they have crossed their minds during the brief time. Make a note of it in this room such that this estimate is visual.

- The last move is a different strategy. Instead of deliberately wanting to block your thoughts, make your client spend the same amount of time thinking about something else they like — tell them to move around or do whatever comes easily. After that, they guess how many times the idea came into their heads. This figure can now be compared to the model in the previous stage.

2) Recognizing emotional avoidance approaches worksheet

Emotional avoidance is another successful technique that people prefer to employ as they come up with uncomfortable thoughts or emotions. Avoiding short-term feelings can appear beneficial, but over the longer term, it reinforces the apparent tolerability of specific mental interactions. Therapists should interact with people to understand that they are cognitively attempting to escape anxiety by typical behaviors such as distraction or rumination. This practice is better performed after you have applied the idea of emotional (or experiential) avoidance to your patient. If you indulge yourself in this exercise, you will find a valuable theoretical context and examples to get you started.

   a. Start by remembering any of your past experiences, where

you prevented an unpleasant emotion, occurrence, or recollection, rather than acknowledgment or participation.

b. Think of different realms of your life whether it helps, whether at work, with your family, or with your friends. You could have played video games instead of having a serious conversation about something that upsets you. Or, you may have turned down an excellent new job at work because it included public speaking.

c. Everything you remember, write down the answers while you focus on three things:

- Perceptions about your experience dreamed up (Difficult Emotions)

- How you sought to suppress certain emotions, psychologically or by those actions (Emotional Avoidance Strategy)
- The degree to which the prevention was useful (Result / Effectiveness)

'Being aware' is one of the most complicated and central elements of mindfulness. In the ACT, as noted, the goal is to acknowledge what we feel without over-inflating or over-identifying it. Being honest with our mental experiences allows us to build space for ideas, thoughts, and emotions that exist in nature as a natural part of life.

3) Five senses worksheet

Starting with some simple mindfulness techniques is a successful approach if your client is not comfortable with the term. The Five Senses Worksheet provides a quick, realistic series that helps you to become conscious of what's right here right now.

- First, you consider five things you see. Instead of being wrapped up in thoughts or thinking processes that may sound daunting, attempt to tune in visually – what's out of your head?
- Second, by moving your mind to four things you can experience. Gently shift the mind away from internal processes and start hearing sounds that you would otherwise not have paid attention to it. When you venture more and more into a state of mindfulness, we will become more disconnected from unpleasant thoughts or stressful emotions.
- Try to remember three things that you can hear.
- You can smell two things.

- Finally, concentrate on one thing that you can taste at this particular moment in time. As you slowly bring this mini-exercise to a close, try to recall how you feel this meditative state if you think over-identifying with your feelings or emotions during the day.

Being present is very useful in appreciating what is unfolding rather than just in our minds. It empowers us to contribute to larger ambitions rather than to get wrapped up in past events and internal changes while improving our potential to embrace and resolve our challenges. We have a wide variety of mindfulness activities that you can browse and choose one if you like; they're going to benefit your client or your practice.

Cognitive diffusion worksheets

4) From cognitive convergence to diffusion worksheet

Cognitive diffusion exercises are intended to address the perceived (sometimes overwhelming) integrity of painful cognitions and emotions. Keeping feelings like "I'm bad" or "I'm worthless" so simply makes it much harder for one to see them as what they are to see feelings as thoughts. This ACT Cognitive Diffusion Worksheet from our more comprehensive Toolkit offers further insight into how the technique can be used with more adaptive ways of responding to psychological interactions.

- Start by defining an ineffective or hurtful self-criticism that you or your client would like to diffuse, such as "I'm a careless spouse." It can be difficult to express at first but strive to

77

shorten it to a sentence that gets to the heart of the matter.

- Let yourself connect with and genuinely contribute to the thinking you have described. It could help if you verbalize the sentence you landed on or repeat it mentally.

- Then, replay the thought, but precede it with "I think that," so the statement can become "I think that I'm a careless spouse."

- We take another mental step back to diffuse this idea further. This time, the unpleasant thinking starts with "I notice I have the feeling that" so, "I notice I 'm having the thought that I'm a carefree spouse."

- Give yourself a chance to focus on the mental change that is sure to have taken place, or at least has begun. How can you characterize the feeling as you've progressed from 'fusion with' to 'diffusion from' the thought?

Self as context worksheet

5) The observer worksheet

More realistic activities also help you learn to be an observer of one. As an example, one instance of being an Observer can look like this:

- Think of the roles you play every day — are you a mother? Are you a master at work? Are you a squad player, sometimes? Are you a daughter? Are you a caregiver? Even if we don't knowingly carry on a role in the world around us, we do. And yet, throughout this changing position, a part of us remains constant.

- The Spectator self means that the positions you have established are not defined; instead, it is the constant that can see the changes take place. The Spectator is seeing what you're doing, thinking, and hearing, and just seeing.

- As your Observer, watch, listen, and note any turbulence that you would otherwise cause to absorb or describe. Note how these perceptions are continually changing, and strive to let go. Recognize that the 'you' stay intact.

Values explanation worksheet

6) Problems and values

Researchers say that we should think of two essential groups when it comes to minimizing struggle and misery in our lives. We may also use two similarly categories critical to learn about how to create a positive, rich experience. Using these four categories, think about and write down your thoughts and feelings. Problem Feelings and Emotions: What self-criticisms, worries, feelings, emotions, memories, or other ideas seem to preoccupy you? List any of the thoughts, sensations, or sentiments that you find difficult to cope with it.

Problem Behaviors: explain some of the acts you take that are detrimental to things over time:

- Save your energy, time, or financial resources.
- Prevent you from moving forward in your life
- Hold you away from activities you'd like to do

Values: List particular stuff that matters to you individually in the long term. What of your strengths and attributes would you like to draw on? What stuff do you (or do you want to) stand for? And what ways do you expect to go forward by tackling your problems? What are some of the ways you'd like to improve or enhance your relationship?

Goals and Actions: List any of your existing habits or actions that are intended to improve your life in the longer term. What is that stuff you'd like to do, more or new things you'd like to do? Can you think about any of the moves you want to take to better your life? Skills that you plan to draw on?

7) Principles worksheet

This conversation sheet, resource, or handout presents a framework that clients can use to analyze and focus on their personal beliefs. As well as helping them (or you) gets some insight, they stimulate thought about future life goals in 10 different ways. After the first few explanations, you would be able to build your questions along the same lines.

Categories and some samples of questions are as follows:

- Romantic Relationships – What kind of partner would you want to be? How are you going to characterize your perfect relationship? What kind of actions are you trying to display towards a significant other?
- Comfort and leisure – What sort of things do you enjoy? When would you like to use your downtime? What's exciting about you? Is it relaxing?
- Job/career – What career aspirations are important to you? What kind of work? Do you aspire to unique qualities as a worker? What kind of

professional relationship would you like to develop?

- Friends – What kind of social ties do you think it is necessary to develop? What do you think is a meaningful social life to have? How do you like your peers to see you as a person?

- Parenthood – What kind of mother or parent do you want to be? Are there specific attributes you'd like to role model for your kids? How would you describe your ideal relationships with them?

- Health and physical wellness – These questions will be based on health goals, ambitions, as well as the importance of personal health, physical well-being, and personal care.

- Interpersonal citizenship / Environmental responsibility – This category is about being part of society, environmental goals and can include humanitarian work.

- Family relationships – Like parenthood above, these values relate to relatives like siblings, extended family, and so forth.

- Spirituality – The relevant questions here are about faith, religious convictions about something important at a broader or broader level.

- Professional development and growth – Reflections in this area can refer to personal abilities, professional skills, knowledge, and growth.

-

8) Worksheets with determined behavior

Commitment, obstructions, and tactics

Commitment is about preserving the drive to continue to achieve the life goals of a client over time. Drawing on goal-setting philosophy, however, helps to provide straightforward, concrete goals with optimistic 'approach' objectives. Using these three headings, build a 3-column grid as follows:

Willingness

In this section, your client designs targets that represent the principles of each of the above activities.

Potential hindrances

Identify potential roadblocks along with each pledge from the list.

Strategies to enhance dedication

So, you will come up with possible alternate routes in this section.

Responsibility, challenges, and approaches

This Exploring Willingness and Dedication worksheet reflect on one attribute that you or your client has defined.

- What worth would you like to add more to your life? Note: this should not be a target but rather something that you or your client personally considers significant and relevant.

- Then select a target that is connected to this value — one that you would like to achieve, and that helps you to measure your success.

- Then, pick one or more acts that you hope would move you closer to the target.

- What sort of personal 'stuff' might be triggered by your committed action? Help to break down this into three areas: a) physical and psychological emotions, b) unproductive/unpleasant self-criticisms or ideas, and c) perceptions and memories.

After focusing on these sections, the emphasis is on the personal 'things.' It's time to frame these as 'things' emotions and thoughts rather than fact, as strong or negative as they can be. And if they happen, we can still do what we're committed to it.

Psychological paradigm versatility

The primary purpose of ACT is to improve psychological resilience, the capacity to contact the present moment more thoroughly as a conscious human being and to alter or continue in action that satisfies the valued ends.

CHAPTER 2: ACCEPTANCE AND COMMITMENT THERAPY (ACT)

Acceptance and Commitment Therapy (ACT) is an action-oriented approach to psychotherapy that is based on classical behavioral therapy and cognitive behavioral therapy. Clients learn to avoid resisting, denying, and dealing with their thoughts and instead recognize that these deeper feelings are acceptable reactions to circumstances that do not hinder them from going on with their lives. With this acknowledgment, clients tend to recognize their struggles and difficulties. They dedicate themselves to making the required adjustments in their actions, regardless of what happens in their life and how they feel about it.

When it is used

ACT has been used effectively to help treat stress at work, test anxiety, generalized anxiety disorder, depression, obsessive-compulsive disorder, and psychotic. It has also been used to treat medical problems such as chronic pain, alcohol misuse, and diabetes.

What to Wait for

Working with a psychiatrist, you can learn how to listen to your self-talk or to talk directly to yourself about stressful experiences, problematic relationships, physical disabilities, or other problems. You will then determine whether an issue needs urgent intervention and change or whether it will — or must — be tolerated for what it is as you learn to make behavioral changes that can impact the situation. You may be looking at what has not worked for you in the past so that the counselor can help you avoid reinforcing cycles of thinking and action that are giving you more problems in the long run.

How it's work

The idea behind ACT is that it is not only successful but also a counter-productive attempt to regulate negative thoughts or psychological events since the repression of these feelings inevitably leads to further discomfort. ACT holds the view that there are legitimate approaches to attempting to modify the way you think, including compassion, devotion to personal values, and dedication to action. By taking action to improve their behavior and, at the same time, trying to recognize their psychological interactions, clients will gradually change their mood and their emotional state. What to look for in Recognition and Dedication Therapist Look for a certified, experienced therapist, social worker, skilled psychologist, or other mental health qualified with additional ACT qualifications. There is no clear qualification for ACT professionals. Skills are learned by peer counseling, seminars, and other teaching programmers. In addition to these skills, it is crucial to choose a therapist with whom you feel comfortable working.

ACT history

Researchers in the field of psychology have worked for decades to create science-based, time-limited treatments for individuals who want to solve mental health problems. As a result, more individuals have had considerable improvement in resolving and handling a variety of issues and report improved well-being as a result. However, long-term recovery and avoidance of relapse remain essential as areas of possible challenge for that pursuing mental health treatment. New forms of therapy, like the ACT, have increasingly been introduced in the hope of improving long-term progress in the treatment of mental health problems. ACT is based on relational structure theory (RFT), a research school focused on human language and cognition. RFT implies that the analytical skills used by the human mind to address problems can be unsuccessful in helping individuals resolve psychological distress. Based on this suggestion, ACT therapy has been created to educate us that, while relational pain is natural, we will learn how to live healthier, better lives by improving the way we think about the problem. In the late 1990s, several detailed recovery manuals have been produced to outline how ACT should be used to treat different mental health disorders. Treatment using these guides has been empirically researched. It has resulted in support for the use of ACT in the treatment of substance abuse, psychosis, anxiety, depression, chronic pain, and eating disorders.

THE principle of ACT interpretation

The principle of ACT does not describe unwanted emotional events as signs or difficulties. Instead, it aims to overcome the propensity of others to see persons needing treatment as disabled or deficient and to make people understand the fullness and resilience of life. This fullness encompasses a wide variety of human experience, including the suffering that will naturally follow such circumstances. Acceptance of situations as they arrive, without evaluating or wanting to alter them, is an ability gained by mindfulness activities in and out of session. ACT does not try to actively change or avoid unwanted emotions or emotions (as cognitive behavioral therapy does) but instead helps people to build a healthy, more caring interaction with these experiences. This change will liberate individuals from challenges seeking to regulate their businesses and make them more responsive to acts compatible with their beliefs; the clarification of thoughts and the definition of values-based priorities are both central components of ACT.

Description and ACT principles

Values clarity will allow people to identify what is most important their values, in other words, and to take constructive action driven by those values. A mental health provider will typically use several activities to help people interested in treatment to recognize the principles selected. These principles also serve as a guideline in the course of deliberate and productive conduct. Exploring unpleasant feelings or overthinking a problem can interfere with one's ability to choose purposeful and valuable action. By conscious freedom from this challenge, ACT will encourage people to act more consistently with their beliefs and to live in a way that feels normal and satisfying.

Who offers the ACT?

The ACT group does not give official credentials to practitioners seeking to practice this method of therapy. The Association for Contextual Behavior Science (ACBS) operates a voluntary list of members who have classified themselves as ACT practitioners, and this list may be a helpful starting point for those involved in seeking an ACT provider.

The ACBS also makes the following recommendations for those involved in seeking an ACT therapist:

- Contact the Department of Psychology, Social Care, or Psychiatry at a local college or university.

Members of the faculty or staff who are specialists in behavioral counseling or cognitive behavioral therapy may know about a nearby ACT therapist.

- Association for Behavioral and Cognitive Therapy offers a directory of providers of behavioral and cognitive therapy. These therapists may provide ACT, or they may know a peer who provides ACT.
- In countries other than the United States, ABCT-like agencies may be a useful resource for practitioners who deliver ACTs or who may refer clients to ACT-trained therapists.

Psychological rigidity

For psychiatrists and other mental health practitioners, the happiness trap is often compatible with the values of ACT. It offers you questions to test your clients for their psychological inflexibility. Psychological inflexibility is the degree to which someone has difficulties practicing six fundamental mechanisms. The questions map to the opposite of the six main processes is as follows:

- The dominance of the conceptualized past or future; limited self-knowledge (as opposed to acceptance)
- Fusion (compared to diffusion)
- Experiential prevention (as opposed to being present)
- Attachment to the conceptualized self (as opposed to self as a context)
- Lack of clarity / correspondence values (vs. values)
- Impractical action (against committed action)

This collection of questions can be a perfect way to help your clients figure out where to concentrate their resources. This is a vital step towards accepting their experiences and working based on their deepest interests.

ACT to cure disabilities

Like mindfulness, ACT can be used in any person's life and can assist with general anxiety disorder, depression, severe pain, addiction, Obsessive-compulsive disorder, eating disorders, and social anxiety disorder.

Disorders of general and social distress

Many studies indicate the beneficial effects of this type of therapy on nervous patients. For example, one study found that college students who were taking ACT therapy reported less stress in academic problems, diminished symptoms of anxiety and depression, increased overall mental health, and strengthened mental acceptance. Another research reinforced these beneficial results on pressure and found that ACT could be as successful as ACT delivered by the therapist. Participants in this study reported decreased general and social anxiety, whether in the "natural care" group or the online ACT group.

Congenital pain

Acceptance and Commitment Therapy has been shown to enhance the quality of living without affecting the level of discomfort experienced in certain forms of chronic suffering. One research found that cancer patients receiving ACT registered substantial changes in recognition of their conditions and the finding of increased significance in life, even though still suffering discomfort. Another research has shown that ACT increases psychological resilience and reduces suicidal symptoms even as chronic pain exists. This result was confirmed by another study, which stated that physical and emotional functioning increased with ACT, even without a concurrent decrease in pain.

Anxiety

Similarly, ACT has been shown to alleviate symptoms for individuals suffering from depression. One research showed the ACT reduced the severity of depressive symptoms in warriors of depression and suicidal thoughts. ACT has decreased psychological inflexibility and agitation due to depression and anxiety in older people, also with a short course from the beginner ACT psychiatrist.

Obsessive-compulsive disorder (OCD)

ACT can also support patients with Obsessive-Compulsive Disorder (OCD). A review of the quantitative studies performed in this field has found that ACT care for OCD is as effective as care as usual, like cognitive behavioral therapy.

Eating Disorders

Finally, ACT was also successfully extended to people with eating disorders. Case-series research on women with eating disorders found that participants progressed by the use of ACT. One woman had reached a point where her symptoms no longer matched the psychiatric concept of disordered eating, although both showed an improvement in their body image flexibility. In a study of people with anorexia, individuals seeking care that involved ACT were more likely to achieve favorable effects at the end of the course.

Applying ACT to group counseling

Acceptance and Commitment Therapy can be applied on an individual basis, but it is often beneficial when implemented by a treatment group. The Association for Contextual Behavioral Sciences accepts the efficacy of group ACT interventions for frustration, depression and general anxiety, social anxiety, chronic pain, and teenagers in distress. Researchers reinforce the effectiveness of group ACT counseling, noting that group practices may offer participants opportunities to communicate and benefit from each other, gain affirmation that they may urgently need, and practice constructive transparency.

Laws of the Group

Set the guidelines for the group (show each group ready to make things work. Do not attempt to "solve" the emotions of another group member. It is not anticipated that discussions within the group can continue outside this framework, etc.) And make sure the participants of the group know they need to be enforced.

Format and structure of the group

Consider if the group is more general or more unique to a problem such as anxiety or depression. Try leading a group with a mindfulness exercise or keeping a simple mindfulness exercise in your back pocket if a member of a group is out of the way.

Experienced Workouts

Don't be afraid to use innovative activities, but be on the lookout for the group members' decisions during the workout.

Conflicts

When a disagreement occurs, which is sure to happen at some stage, first direct the participant of the party to their inner experience. Help them get their emotions back and make the counseling work for them. Be willing to feel pain. Stop the temptation to "rescue" the members of the party from their suffering. As some clinicians suggest, "Don't steal the war," as it is sometimes a crucial aspect of the group's trust-building method.

Acceptance and Commitment Therapy method

Evaluation

A rigorous clinical evaluation requiring a detailed functional analysis of the issue posed. In specific, the intention is to escape reaction and unproductive attempts to monitor experience those results in the inability to pursue valued objectives. The assessment also involves socioeconomic circumstances, past effects on new behaviors. Diagnostic testing is considered less relevant, as are many other psychological treatments. The main emphasis is on the 'workability' of the methods that a person uses to live their lives / solve their problems and the realistic analysis of actual actions, emotions, and feelings.

Case interpretation

Apart from Cognitive Therapy, ACT therapists rarely provide specific case formulas. Instead, the psychiatrist uses metaphors to explain the usual functional traits that the client faces and to ask the client if this concept corresponds with their direct experience. Examples include the sailing boat metaphor, the riders on the bus metaphor, the guy on the cave metaphor, the power struggle with a beast metaphor.

Creative desperation

In this step, you are collaborating with the client to help them examine the 'workability' of the techniques they use. At this point, the critical goal is to evaluate what the client has done, how well it has performed, and to assess whether or not these methods are part of the issue. Central signals are that laboratory management efforts can be part of the dilemma rather than the solution. Other essential reminders are that the client is not broken, only using ineffective methods to live with what life offers (or has given) them. The goal is to realize that more of the same is unlikely to be helpful. This treatment may need to be something innovative and different from what they have done before. And that letting go of unworkable techniques may mean fostering a desire to sit down for what is uncomfortable or unpleasant so that fresh 'living with' methods can be attempted. While this review sheet portrays these three initial phases as distinct stages, they can be well combined, depending on the client and therapist.

Do the job for the ACT

When the client and therapist formed a strong enough working alliance, and agree that what has been before having not performed well. And that the client is ready to pursue something different and let go of fruitless tactics, ACT's essential work is to determine what the clients want to be for (their values) and to make clear plans and actions. As this occurs, the imagination of the client will continue to come up with excuses that this cannot be, tries to escape, and merges with feelings, values, and laws on how life can be done, about the essence of their issues, or themselves and others. They are standing as barriers between a human and his beliefs. We use metaphor, empathy, acceptance modeling, experiential exercises, and mindfulness strategies to try to promote the ability to conquer these challenges just as they are. The goal is to encourage an observant, detached, and accepting attitude towards these obstacles. We use behavioral strategies such as hierarchies and goal-setting, strapping, modeling, role-playing, and practice to try and model, initiate and improve practices that drive an individual towards their valued goals. We use the counseling room to help people differentiate between actions and situations that take them away from their beliefs and to strive to allow them more choice in those moments.

For some clients, we have to start with attributes: what are we heading to be doing this strange thing called therapy? It has to be something that matters to them. Many people are a long way from deciding their life to be, and this work can be painful and sluggish. This also requires a great deal of recognition and diffusion. Both to be in touch with what counts and to encourage the idea that counseling could be about striving with it. Other clients are so amalgamated with thoughts and opinions about themselves. They ought to continue with diffusion, recognition. Diffusion-based strategies

Contrarily to cognitive therapy, ideas are not classified as logical or irrational or skewed or functional or unstable. Instead, we see the interaction that one has with certain feelings as either workable or unworkable at any given time. We don't even get into arguing about how much a client thinks or doesn't believe an idea or opinion, and we especially don't get mixed up in arguing about whether the concept is real or authentic. Instead, we use cognitive and imagery-based techniques, as well as other experiential methods, to help us perceive emotions as thoughts, including those that are very painful. We do this in the service of unraveling thoughts as motives for action. So that decisions are more consistently governed by the preference of the person of their beliefs, rather than by what their 'minds' tell them they should be doing. We refer to the mind as the subconscious to differentiate the reason from the self. We point out the language development, such as the past of a word, in an attempt to see words as terms, even when it comes to complicated things. We use bodily movements and photographs to characterize thoughts and opinions as part of the self but distinct from the self.

Values dependent interference

Although many people may set goals for themselves in some areas of life, many of us live with an unconscious understanding of what is important to us. Other ways to express this are, "What do we want to do? What's most important to us? "For many people, life is so far away from these thoughts that they feel relatively unfamiliar and very dangerous. For us, life is about doing as we're told, what's expected of us, what's in line with our positions. This can be so much in many parts of lives, we are not even mindful of choosing, or that choice even exists. Even people who work very well in the field may not have accepted this part of their life (including the people we call therapists). In this phase of the work, we are seeking to help people make immediate experiential communication with the following questions: What do I want to stand for here? If I had to pick, what would my life be like? What truly matters to me? We do this by imaging exercises, sitting on the issue and discussing it, and also through the paradoxical technique of looking at what is unpleasant or prevented. Values and vulnerabilities are squeezed out of the same vessel: we see what is precious in our suffering. It's often about being in contact with other people, knowing like we belong and are loved like we make a difference to the people around us, that we matter, that we care for people in our lives, that we contribute in any way to the world around us.

We're trying to help a person make meaningful interaction with this in their lives, and counseling is being entirely in the service of enjoying a valued life with less difficulty. Usually, this would mean dealing skillfully with the challenges that would very inevitably emerge when an individual moves, letting go of tactics that don't perform, encouraging clients to be able to have whatever pops about when they progress towards principles. Part of the work may be to create specific behavioral targets following certain directions and to split them into small steps to allow a sequence of smaller movements to make larger movements. The feelings, memories, and values the client has been dealing with are going to have along for the adventure.

Meditative Stance of ACT

It should be evident from this overview that the clinical role in the ACT is one of equity. All psychiatrist and clients are human beings that have thoughts. They are both people who, at times, have known hardship, heartache, pleasure, sorrow, longing, and pain. They're both people who have behaved in ways that they regret or were not their best selves, and they both get wrapped up in the laws of how we 'should' behave and what we 'should' do at any given time. The ACT Therapist welcomes this mutual humanity and seeks to create equity in the relationship. This may include chosen self-disclosure in the service of the client's principles or struggles. Effective ACT therapist is likely to develop a reflective, defused, flexible space in which everything can be explored in the room, particularly the problems of the process as to what is in the place. To be witnessed by all sides, in the here and now. At about the same time, the ACT counselor is essentially prescriptive or directing so that they are more effective in the service of the cherished life of the person.

Clients can require a lot of motivation and psychological influence to give up old habits, do new activities, and sit down with tough stuff. The ACT therapist is active and goal-oriented. The objective is to sit happily with painful material, and the therapist may sit softly, empathizing, encouraging gently, allowing the room for emotion to be fully present, and helping the client to develop an agreed, accommodating, defused, and presently centered attitude towards the painful material. If, on the other hand, the immediate therapy aim is to make a challenging thought lighter, the therapist can be playful, using laughter, using games and activities to encourage the person to feel the thought as a thought and maybe very provocative towards the thinking. This will rely on the client and the essence of the partnership. And will never be achieved in a spirit of disrespecting the client or acting irreverently towards them. The ACT paradigm is evident in that therapists should do a fair deal of experiential learning on how the models and strategies are applied to their own lives. ACT teaching is also extremely experiential, and those pursuing additional training should expect to be in contact with challenging content in their own lives during training.

Foundation of evidence

The ACT group is committed to a rigorous evaluation of the results of ACT in clinical trials and laboratory research. Two primary studies discuss the result literature and the fundamental evidential basis of the ACT. Several other reviews have been performed outside the ACT community. These external assessments have been more critical of the empiric status of the ACT, citing methodological limitations in a variety of ACT action reports. Data shows the ACT is useful in chronic pain, stress, anxiety, asthma, diabetes, paranoia, and tinnitus, and irritable bowel syndrome— children with intellectual disorders, Obsessive-compulsive disorder, and drug abuse. And smoke abstinence, anxiety testing, Post-traumatic stress disorder, end-stage cancer, and adolescents with stress.

The practices

ACT can be provided independently, in groups, by organized self-help workbooks, in conventional 50-minute sessions or brief appointments, and a 2 + 1 model. These factors depend on the service, the customer, and the essence of the issues. The ACT model is versatile, and new strategies can be quickly built based on its concepts.

CHAPTER 3: FORMULATION OF THE ACT CASE STRUCTURE

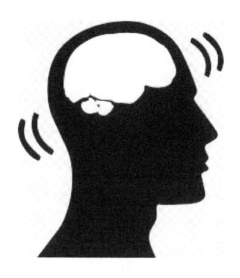

1. Context for the description of the situation

The purpose of ACT is to help clients regularly continue to act successfully (concrete actions following their values) in the face of challenging or destructive private events.

2. Decision Tree on assessment and care

Starting with the target issue as defined by the client or significant others, simplify these complaints and problems into functional solution groups that are sensitive to the formulation of the ACT and the contextual conditions of the client, and relate the care components to that framework.

A. Consider general behavioral themes and habits, client experience, current life situation, and session actions that could be important to the practical understanding of particular goals in ACT terminology.

They may include:

- General type of experiential prevention (core inappropriate feelings, perceptions, memories, etc.; what are the implications of experiencing interactions that the client does not want to risk)
- The extent of explicit behavioral avoiding is seen (what areas of the life the client has fallen out of)
- Degree of actively mediated cognitive management techniques (i.e., psychological stimulation, destructive self-instruction, intense self-monitoring, dissociation, etc.)
- Degree of external mental management techniques (drinking, consuming drugs, smoking, self-mutilation, etc.)
- Loss of life direction (general lack of values; aspects of the patient's life

"checked out" such as marriage, home, self-care, spiritual)

- The fusion of the assessment of opinions and logical categories (domination of "right and wrong" even though it is harmful; high degrees of reasoning; the uncommon value of "understanding" etc.)

B. Evaluate the future roles of these targets and their therapeutic effects.

1. Is this goal related to the basic implementation of the patterns laid out in "A" above?

2. If so, what are the primary material realms and aspects of avoided private activities, the feared effects of witnessing avoided private events, the convergence of feelings, motives, and interpretations, and the feared impacts of defusing held thinking or regulations.

3. If so, in what other behavioral domains do you see the same functions?

4. Are there other, more direct, roles that are also involved (e.g., social assistance, financial implications)?

5. Because of the functions listed, what are the possible relative contributions of:

   a. Inventive hopelessness (clients still oblivious to the unworkable existence of the reform agenda).
   b. Understanding that unreasonable attempts at regulation are an issue (the patient does not feel the paradoxical consequences of law).
   c. Experienced interaction with the non-toxic essence of private activities by acceptance and disclosure (the client is unable to isolate himself from reactions, memories, negative thoughts).

d. Developing desire (Client is reluctant to alter actions because of belief).

e. Consequences in tackling the feared events).

f. Participating in committed action based on principles (the client does not have a substantial life) Plan and wants support to rediscover a value-based way of life).

C. Evaluate the reasons that can reinforce the use of ineffective improvement methods and recovery outcomes.

1. Client's record of follow-up and correctness (if this is a problem, consider confronting purpose by diffusion strategies; pit being right versus the cost to strength; consider the need for self-context and mindfulness practice to minimize attachment to a conceptualized self).

2. Degree of conviction on the overall viability of those tactics (if this is a problem, assume the need to disrupt the wrongly focused agenda for reform, i.e., imaginative hopelessness).

3. Believing that improvement is not necessary (if this is a problem, consider diffusion strategies; reconsider the cost of not trying; arrange behavioral experiments)

4. Fear of the effects of the transition (if this is a problem, thought acceptance, disclosure, and diffusion).

5. The short-term result of ultimately unworkable reform tactics is optimistic (consider value work if this is an issue).

D. Find the general strengths and deficiencies of the client and the actual client context.

1. Social, financial, and technical services needed to activate for therapy

2. Lifeskills (if this is a concern, consider those that will need to be tackled by first-order reform initiatives such as relaxation, cognitive skills, time management, and personal problem - solving skills)

E. Consider the inspiration for progress and the reasons that may adversely affect it.

1. "Cost" of goal activities in terms of day-to-day functioning (if this is poor or not adequately contacted, think paradox, attention, evocative exercises before work that assume substantial personal motivation).

2. Experience of poorly oriented improvement attempts (if this is poor,

switch straight to the regular appraisal of the workability of the struggle, to experiments intended to measure it or, if it does not work, to the referral).

3. Clarity and significance of valued ends that are not reached due to functional goal actions and their position in the more significant set of values of the client (if this is low, as is always the case, consider the consistency of values. If it is essential for the recovery process itself, consider setting the values for character earlier in the treatment process).

4. Power and value of the therapeutic interaction (if not optimistic, strive to establish, e.g., by self-disclosure; if optimistic, consider incorporating ACT reform with direct help and input during the session).

F. Find positive behavioral improvement reasons.

1. Degree of insight and awareness (if understanding is encouraged, passes through early stages to more experiential phases; if it is not enabled, consider confronting purpose through diffusion strategies; compare being correct versus the cost to vitality; consider the need for self-context and mindfulness practice to minimize attachment to a conceptualized self).

2. Past expertise in addressing related challenges (if they are constructive and healthy from an ACT standpoint, consider going immediately to reform initiatives that are unnecessarily modeled after previous successes).

3. Previous sensitivity to mindfulness/spirituality ideas (if they are

constructive and healthy from an ACT standpoint, consider relating these interactions to change efforts; if they are nasty or dangerous – such as comparing spirituality with dogma, consider developing self-context and mindfulness skills).

Building interventions on the approach of life improvement and transition:

A. Established particular priorities in line with the general principles

B. Take steps and contact obstacles

C. Dissolve obstacles through recognition and diffusion

D. Repeat and make assumptions in different domains

Fast and straightforward ACT analysis of psychiatric issues

Psychological disorders are due to a lack of behavioral stability and efficacy. The shortage of repertoires originates from history and habit, but in particular from cognitive fusion and its multiple consequences, along with the subsequent aversive regulation mechanisms. The first of these consequences was the prevention and exploitation of private activities. "Conscious regulation" is a question of orally controlled behavior. It is mainly in the field of transparent, analytical actions, not automated and elicited functions. Clients are not broken because, in the areas of recognition and diffusion, they have the necessary social tools they need to learn the expertise they need. The value of any action is its strength and durability evaluated against the actual costs of the patient (that he/she would have had if he/she were chosen). Values define the types of productivity required and, thus, the essence of the problem. A psychiatric job, therefore, needs clarity of principles. We have to let go of an existing one to take a new path. If the dilemma is recurrent, the treatments of clients are probably part of it. When you see unusual loops, it includes incorrect verbal rules. The bottom-line problem is living well, and feeling good, not feeling excellent.

The act therapeutic position

Assume that drastic, powerful transformation is inevitable and that whatever the client faces, it is not the enemy. It's the battle against experiences that are negative and painful. You can't save your clients from the complexity and challenge of growth. Compassionately, do not recognize the grounds for this — the concern is whether it is workable or not appropriate. If the client is stuck, irritated, puzzled, frightened, furious, or eager to be happy — this is just what needs to be done, and it's here now. Turn the obstacle to the potential. If you feel trapped, irritated, puzzled, frightened, and angry or worried, be happy: you're in the same boat as the client, and that can idealize your job. In the field of recognition, diffusion, ego, and beliefs, it is more critical as a psychiatrist to do what you say than to say what you agree over. Don't be persuaded. It's about the client's life and the client's experience, not the thoughts and values. Belief is not a friend of yours. Your brain is not a friend of yours. It's not your adversary, either. It's the same for your customers. You're on the same aircraft. Never cover yourself by moving a client up. The problem is always a function, not a shape or a frequency. When in question, ask yourself or the customer, "What's that in the service of."

Therapeutic measures ACT

Be passionately interested in what the client wants compassionately confront unworkable agendas. Always acknowledging the client's perspective as a good therapist helps the client to feel and think about what they believe and suppose explicitly, as it is not what they think it is, and to reach a place where it is possible to do so. Support the client in a respected way, with both their history and automatic reactions. Enable the client to detect pits, mergers, and odd loops and to embrace, defuse, and step in a respected path. That creates more extensive and broader trends of successful action Repeat, extend the field of work, and repeat before clients generalize. Don't believe a thing you say or me either.

Core ACT skills

Main requirements associated with basic ACT therapy posture

Collectively, the following characteristics describe the fundamental clinical role of ACT.

- The psychiatrist talks to the client from an equal, insecure, sincere, and common point of view and acknowledges the client's innate capacity to transition from unworkable to successful responses.

- The therapist consciously models both the acknowledgment of uncomfortable material (e.g., what occurs through treatment) and the ability to retain conflicting or complicated thoughts, emotions, or memories.

- The psychiatrist allows the client to come into touch with actual reality and does not try to save the client from traumatic therapeutic material.

- The psychiatrist should not argue, lecture, intimidate, or try to persuade the client of something.

- The therapist uses experiential drills, paradoxes, and metaphors as necessary and de-emphasizes the literal "sense-making" when debriefing.

- The psychiatrist can make self-disclosures about personal matters before making a psychological argument.

- The therapist approach and create creative metaphors, experiential activities, and therapeutic activities to suit tailors the client's experience, language usage, and psychological, cultural, and racial meaning.

- The therapist can use the actual space of the counseling setting to model ACT posture (e.g., sitting side by side, using items in the room to represent the ACT concept visually).

- The applicable ACT procedures are understood at the moment and, where appropriate, are assisted explicitly in the sense of the clinical partnership.

Critical skills for ACT key procedures and clinical intervention

Developing Recognition and Willingness / Undermining Experimental Regulation

- The therapist expresses that the client is not broken but uses unworkable methods.

- Psychiatrist allows the person to have eye contact with the paradoxical effect of stress management techniques.
- Counsellor actively incorporates the idea of "workability" in therapeutic interactions.
- The therapist consciously urges the client to experiment with avoiding the battle for moral dominance and recommends willingness as an option.
- The therapist emphasizes the distinction between the workability of influence and willingness techniques (e.g., variations in vitality, intent, or meaning).
- Psychiatrist lets the individual examine the connection between the extent of willingness and suffering (voluntary suffering; clean and dirty suffering).

- The therapist allows the person to make experiential communication with the expense of not being eager compared to cherished ends of life (doing the values, listing worth, need for emotional control, payment, short-term/long-term costs and benefits).
- The therapist allows the client to experience the attributes of willingness (choice, actions, lack of will, the same intervention, no matter how high the stakes).
- The therapist should use activities and metaphors to show the ability to act in the face of challenging content (e.g., hopping, lap cards, a box full of things)
- A therapist can use a standardized and directly proportionate to eager assignments.

- Therapist models willingness in the counseling interaction and lets the client generalize this ability to events beyond the therapy setting (e.g., bringing the therapist's negative responses to the workshop material of the room, exposing events in the therapist's own life that involved a willingness to act).

Undermining behavioral consolidation

- The therapist may encourage the person to get in touch with attachments to mental, cognitive, behavioral, or physical boundaries and the effect of the association on motivation.
- The therapist consciously compares what the client's "mind" suggests is working to what the client's experience means is using.

- The therapist uses vocabulary conventions, metaphors, and experiential activities to build a separation between the client's actual reality and his / her conceptualization of that perception (e.g., getting off our buttocks, bubble on the back, tin can is a monster).
- The therapist uses several interventions that both show that unnecessary private encounters are not toxic and should be embraced without judgment.
- The therapist uses a combination of drills, symbols, and mental tasks to expose the programmed and literal properties of language and thoughts.
- The therapist helps the client illustrate the client's "narrative" while emphasizing the possibly unworkable consequences of literal plot

attachment (e.g., appraisal vs. explanation, autobiography revision, good cup / bad cup).

- The therapist senses fusion during the consultation and helps the client to detect it.

Keeping in touch with the current moment

- The therapist should defuse the content of the client and guide focus to the moment.
- Therapist models that allow contact with and communicate emotions, ideas, memories, or perceptions at a time within a therapy relationship;
- The therapist uses activities to increase the client's understanding of experience as an evolving phase.
- Clinicians monitor session material at various levels (e.g., verbal actions,

body posture, and emotional shifts) and stress that they are there while it is helpful.

- Therapist models going out of the "mind" and going back to the current moment.

Differentiating the conceptualized identity from the context of self

- Physician-assisted, the client distinguishes between self-assessment and self-evaluation (thank your brain for that thinking, calling thinking, naming a case, selecting an identity).
- The therapist uses mindfulness meditation (that you call; chessboard, parade soldiers/leaves on the stream) to help the person make communication with self-as-context.
- The therapist uses metaphors to illustrate the difference between goods

and contents of cognition versus consciousness itself (furniture at home, are you strong enough to have you).

- The therapist uses therapeutic tasks (take your head for a walk) to help the client practice different private experiences from self-awareness.
- The therapist allows the person to have direct communication with the three components of self-experience (e.g., self-conceptualization, constant phase of knowledge, transcendent self-experience).

Defining the valid directions

- A therapist can help clients explain valued life paths (value assessment, value clarity exercise, what do you want your life to stand for, funeral exercise).

- The therapist encourages the client to "go on records" as advocating for the precious life.
- The therapist can state his / her values as they apply to therapy and is diligent not to replace the importance of the client.
- The psychiatrist helps clients to differentiate between beliefs and objectives.
- The therapist distinguishes between goals (outcomes) and the mechanism of striving towards goals (growth that happens as a result of striving).
- The therapist respects the client's principles, and, whether he or she is not able to comply with them, directs the client to another provider or group resource.

Develop the habits of intervention

- The therapist allows the individual to set targets based on value and to create a clear action plan.

- The therapist allows the client to differentiate between determining and preferring to participate in the determined intervention.

- The therapist helps the person to make and sustain promises in the face of potential obstacles (e.g., fear of loss, painful experiences, sadness).

- The therapist encourages the person to recognize the effect that "right" could have on the desire to meet responsibilities (e.g., fish hook metaphor, acceptance, that's going to be right, how your story is going to keep you healthy).

- The therapist encourages the client to anticipate and be able to have any potential obstacles that occur as a result of participating in dedicated acts.

- Irrespective of the scale of the action, the therapist allows the person to understand the unique attributes of committed action (e.g., increased vitality, a feeling of going forward rather than backward, growing rather than shrinking)

- The therapist allows the individual to develop greater and greater patterns of successful intervention.

- A non-judgmental therapist allows the client to integrate slips or relapses as an essential part of maintaining promises and building successful responses.

A few examples of the attributes of ACT

Facing the present circumstance ('creative hopelessness')/control is a challenge

Purpose: To note that a reform plan is in place and to record the simple unworkability of the system; to label the system as inadequately implemented control strategies; to analyze why it does not work.

Method: Define what the client has been doing to make it easier, analyze whether or not they have already succeeded in the client's experience, and build space for something different to happen.

In certain instances, however, you can skip this step.

Items to avoid: never attempt to persuade the client: their intuition is an absolute arbitrator. The aim is not a feeling condition; it is what the spiritual tradition called "to be cornered."

Examples of strategies intended to improve artistic hopelessness

1. Innovative distress
Are they able to accept that there may be another way, but they don't need to know?

2. What has taken you into treatment?
Offer a feeling of being trapped in meetings, life being off direction, etc.

3. People in the Whole workout
Demonstrate that they're trying something, and that doesn't work.

4. Chinese Analogy handcuffs

No matter how many times they're trying to pull to get rid of them, moving in is what it takes.

5. Noting the Battle

Tug of war with a demon; the objective is to drop the chain, not to win the war.

6. Driving with the Back-view Mirror

Even if control techniques are taught, that doesn't mean they're working.

7. Clear the old way to make room for the latest

Place filled with dead plants that need to be burned down to allow new trees to flourish.

8. Let down the outdated list

"Isn't it exactly like you? Isn't that familiar to you? Is there anything that one feels old about it?

9. Fallacy

Informing the client their dissatisfaction is a positive result.

10. Feedback Screech Metaphor

It's not the distortion that's the problem, and it's the modulation.

11. The Phenomenon of Controls

"If you're not ready to get it, you've got it."

12. Illusion in Power Metaphor

Fall in love, candy doughnut, what do the numbers work out?

13. Power Effects

Background investigation Metaphor

14. Willingness v/s control

Metaphor on two scales

CHAPTER 4: HOW TO RECLAIM YOUR LIFE?

How to restore your strength & reclaim your life?

Powerless – the sensation that happens when we're in a wrong position, but we don't see some feasible options for change, or we can't see anyway. If we see solutions or escape, they seem unlikely, and we lack the confidence, the resources, and the means to take action. We may have tried to improve the situation in the past with little to no success, or we may have tried to get out, but we were defeated, and finally, in resignation, we said, "This is just how things are." Yet deep down, we're desperate for and ready for improvement. We're having a dream of a new life. We seem to look at others, mainly social media, and fall into "compare and despair." We think, "Man! Look how fantastic they look and how well they're doing! I am such a loser, man!

Quick track for emotional exhaustion

Force ourselves into hardship as we try to "survive" every day when yearning for a new life is beginning to fade. It's an easy way to flame out. Since we feel helpless, instead of making some positive progress, we get trapped. We can't see the trees in the forest. They can't grasp that familiarity is the mental equivalent of protection. When suffering is known, it feels safe. When feeling good about us and leading a vibrant life sound strange, our nervous system considers them as hazardous. The situation continues to rob our vital energy, which is putting a burden on our physical and mental well-being. We lose our strength and become frustrated and resentful. Eventually, these emotions are cascaded into sadness and anxiety.

What kind of script does the nervous system follow?

The more we engage with this trend, the stronger our neurology develops. This standard way of living becomes the script of living that our nervous system reads every day. The writing might sound like, "My life and health are going to suck. I've had too many crappy things to happen outside of my reach. I've been given a lousy deck of cards, so the world must be against me. I am helpless to change my condition because I am too ill, too broken, too reliant on my husband, too frightened, my children, etc. I've done a lot of things that never worked out before, so why bother?

If we continue to improvise this scenario, or something similar, in our heads, we sink further into a pit of misery and helplessness. We're in full-blown burnout or close to it! And we're going around and around until we can't go any further. When we come to the stage where we can't go any forward, we get to the crossroads. This is where we have a significant, life-influencing decision to make. We may resolve to welcome the terror, difficulty, and pain involved in making a transition, or we may allow the suffering of familiarity to overtake us and continue to rob our strength and control.

1) Presume 100 % responsibility for yourself and your happiness

This is the first and most critical step towards a healthier body, mind, and life. You're 100 % responsible for your recovery, no matter what happens in the past. Absorb it and acknowledge it. Enable that way of thought to reinforce your devotion to yourself. Stay concerned about this! Stay respectful. It's half a fight to notice. Note with the same emotional reaction as you would have in a gallery looking at an exciting exhibition. You might say to yourself, "Wow, that's fascinating. I want to learn more." Curiosity is a powerful weapon. You can only change what you're eager and ready to notice.

2) Realize how to adapt to what's going on in your life generates the effects you're getting

Situations arise, and life is always a struggle. It hurts at some point for everyone, but it is our reaction to our condition that affects us more than the situation itself. We do have the power of how we want to react, even though we don't have control over what happened.

3) Deep healing and achievement in life are based on clarity, purpose, commitment, persistence, and action, no matter how little

We want significant improvements, and we need to finish this season of our lives right now! We want to wake up tomorrow, and we want to change something, and we want to do all this hardship. I understand, but even if the significant, drastic shift happened to you today, you'd still be right where you are. You'd slip down the same downward trap that you've caught up in before because the little changes are what give us new independence, the wisdom that we need, and clarity that creates a happier life. Don't underestimate the things you do daily, those things that don't seem big enough to make a difference. Learn to watch for, notice, and enjoy the little changes that happen every day.

4) The fastest and only path of resistance is through it

You're going to meet opposition, and it's mainly from inside. Your desire for improvement and development is perhaps the most frightening aspect of being on the right path. Staying down the same path that got you ill is not going to take you to a way out. We're trying to sprint in the other direction because we're on edge and because our nervous system is trapped in a sympathetic mode of response or fight or flight. You ought to stay still as the opposition arrives and go to the other side of it. There's no short cut through this challenging aspect of your recovery. The good news is that this part of retrieval is often, if ever, the horrible thing that we dread in our minds. You're more likely to find yourself enjoying the process and thinking to yourself, "What was I so frightened of?"

5) Your mind may be either your most excellent companion or your biggest enemy

Your mind is the best tool you've got in your artillery against chronic disease. It can also be the most significant vulnerability in the security mechanism. Work on your mind, and you're going to find your way through. What do you have to lose by trying?

6) Thoughts drive feelings

Feelings are guiding movement or inaction. Performance or omission was turned into routines and patterns. Our impressions are generated through practices and behaviors. Experiences are causing thoughts and perceptions. And we're going around and around. This idea is self-explanatory, but it would help if you take the time to place it in your mind. Try to catch yourself in the process of pattern or habit, and then notice where your thoughts and emotions take you. Try to stop the practice. And we're going back to be curious. Remember how this step-by-step pattern works in your life, and you've got the beginning of the solution! You'll want to change it after you find it. You may also notice that you feel some hope.

7) How we think and respond will either promote or hinder our recovery and fulfillment in life

Take a step back and look at your life as if you were watching a film of your own. If you watch yourself act on your script, what would you say the end of the story would depend on the actions of this hero or heroine? Does it enable you to see a pattern of thinking or action that needs to be observed first, then disrupted, then changed?

8) Remember the theory of Pareto 80/20

80% of our outcomes come from 20% of our actions. Choose your efforts carefully. Failure is a failure if you want to be. If you're going to grow and learn from defeat, it's a victory.

9) Every success is founded on a mountain of assumed "failures."

Features we see as failures are sometimes not "failures" at all. Build space in your life for learning and developing, and not being great. When you're exhausted, you ought to build this room for yourself in particular. Is this sense of failure part of the problem?

10) You're going to get what you tolerate in life

People seem to treat us and react to us by what we accept and how we treat ourselves. This is representative of our life circumstances as well. For example, suppose we stick in a profession, a marriage, or something that drains us because we are too scared to make a change because there are too many difficult challenges to conquer. In that case, we can continue to experience what we don't want to share.

11) Indeed, your life draws your community

The energy you put into the world is the energy you draw to your life. We're energetic beings. And we send off vibrations as active creatures. When you had two tuning forks next to each other, but you just reached one of them, the other will start to vibrate, too. That's precisely how electricity functions. When you go about your day, the energy you bring out is going to resonate with you. When you focus on all of these concepts in this list, you can begin to see some adjustments that take place in response to your very distinct energies resonating through you.

12) Energy goes where you want to go

Intentions are like the ruler of life. When you set your goal in a direction, the whole ship starts to sail in that direction. You can set your intentions more significant and smaller, and you can update them, change them, and reset them as much as you want.

13) What others think about us and see us is none of our concern, nor does it affect or determine our meaning until we allow it to do so

Chronic disease also comes with a lot of individuals who have thoughts on where we've landed, what we're doing with it, and who we are. This can also be one of the most challenging parts of being chronically ill. It's normal to hear rumors from family, mates, and employers who suggest you're not that sick, or that you imagine, or that you can see an extraordinary doctor, and so on. The fact is nothing you do or say is going to affect what they think. They're not describing you as a human. You're going to have to represent yourself. The quicker you begin to express yourself, the better you simplify the entire process of moving towards health. It's all the baggage that needs to be stripped, so you're able to get to work.

14) Searching for acceptance, affirmation, or agreement from others does not serve us in any way. It's just draining us

This principle is the other side of the coin above. On the one side, people decide what they're going to say, and you can't regulate or discourage them from doing it. Still, however, we're going to need validation to feel better about ourselves. It's typically nothing but the fact that you just allowed someone to manipulate your emotions for yourself. You're precious because you're human. Nobody gives you more or less worth regardless of their views. Cultivate a value approach. Dream of who you are, how you want to be, and who you want to be in the future. Create a list of the things you want to do with your life. There are a lot of ways to cultivate the worth you owe yourself. You're in charge of this topic and have absolute control of it.

15) Feeling irritated, discouraged, and burnt out is no indication of giving up—the cues to take a rest and calm down

This is also the hardest thing to be taught by many people. Do you have a long list of unpleasant voices that remind you that you're lazy when you lie down in the afternoon? Are you asking yourself that you "should" be doing extra today because you didn't do enough yesterday? Are you scared that you might never get back up if you lie down? We are mission managers of ourselves, and sometimes we don't even know that we're doing it. Learn to let yourself have a moment of relaxing and reuniting while you feel beaten down! You're going to wake up ready to go again if you're going to give yourself this time. Many of us who have slipped into the severe disease has passed all of our slow-down signs. It's time to listen to what the body is trying to suggest.

16) Shift and recovery take place in the comfort zone

This is real, and the transition will still feel awkward because it's fresh and unexpected. A comfort zone is also simply an old habit that no longer fits us. It can also be a very unproductive cycle of thinking or activity in life, so we keep doing it because it's familiar. This problem might be more complicated than you may expect. Our personality is related to our modes of thinking and our everyday routines. Changing these habits will make you feel like you're losing yourself. If you're waiting for an awkward feeling, it's replaced by curiosity and expectation. To cure, you need to recognize and alter habits that have contributed to sickness. This also allows you to be courageous and ready to cast out everything that no longer fits you.

17) You're the solution to your prayers

No matter what your living conditions are and what they were triggered by, changing the course of your wellness and life starts with you. I have also characterized my long struggle with chronic illness as "falling into the rabbit hole of chronic disease." It sounds like you've been falling and losing control for weeks, months, and even years to come. These concepts work against the massive pull of gravity in your dropping. Or, you might feel like you're flattened on the pavement right now, and gravity might feel safe and familiar. It'll keep you in one place for a bit, at least. Setting in the warm pavement, even if you're used to it now, isn't quite what you like, nor is it going to get you out of the position you've landed. These values are the lift, the helping hand, the ambulance services who come to pick you up, but you have to reach out and take them into your heart and mind and continue to hang on to them.

15 Amazing ways to fix your life when you're broken

If you're coping with a separation, a career loss, or one of the dozen other life circumstances that can bring the entire world to a halt, it's important to note that life is a set of ups and downs for all of us. While it might seem lonely, the truth is that there isn't one among us that didn't feel like we wanted to pull our stereotypical shit together or like we were "losing it" at any stage. If you're in this position right now, take this as your sign to take a deep breath, take charge. Don't you know how to be optimistic after looking like you're falling apart? Here are 15 ways to start restoring self-esteem and get the pieces back together.

01.Avoid using the term "broken" as a starting point

Your words are important, particularly when you talk to yourself. Instead of looking at yourself as "broken" or "missing" or whatever pessimistic, the self-defeating term comes to mind, realize that you're powerful enough to get out of a not-so-great position. It's not about whom you are than where you are, and that's an essential difference when it comes to creating meaningful change.

02. Create a list of stuff that you ought to stop doing

What's the point of a beautiful new habit if you're already engaging in one that contradicts it? Think about it for a moment: visiting the gym every morning and eating half a cake at night doesn't make a lot of effort. It's the same with anything else in your life. Create a list of things you're making that stand in your way and contribute to changing those knee-jerk habits with something else. When you have a schedule, you can concentrate on what you need to start doing.

03. Stop hating yourself

Commit to being an observer of your life, not to judge anything too negatively. Instead of lamenting the things you have done wrong, are thankful for a new outlook and freedom of responsibility, and start working on learning experiences and finding healthier ways to do better.

04. Adjust the conversation

It's relaxing to sit down and rehash the same tales over and over, but our thoughts become our motto, and to mention how sad, broken, or miserable you are would just deepen your feeling of helplessness. Try to use more optimistic and emphatic terms, and you will discover that not only do you feel better, but the world will respond differently to you.

05. Encircle yourself with fighters

Sadness might love company, but do you want to devote the rest of your life hanging out with people who just perpetuate the impression that you are a victim with no personal power? The answer should be no. Surround yourself with people who have a "can-do" mentality towards adversity, and you will not only feel inspired but learn very realistic ways to make changes to your own life.

06. Get a supporter

Contact a trustworthy friend, family member, or therapist to check-in and keep you responsible for achieving your targets every week. Maybe that means you set three goals and then share how you met them or what held you back, or perhaps you're messaging a friend instead of an ex. Whatever it is, getting someone to check in on will help add knowledge to times where you feel like you're sinking.

07. Do some research

It's a simplistic phrase, but awareness is strength. Getting a real sense of what you're going through will make you feel less alone and give you a viewpoint when you're going down an old track. For example, understand the science behind a relationship and how it affects the brain. Will make you understand why the ex's ghosting hurts so badly (thus making you less likely to customize it or compulsively reach out), and reading up on anything like a persistent addiction will bring behavior into context.

08. Take great care of yourself

Small measures in self-care will go a long way to building self-image and boosting trust. Give yourself a facial at home when listening to your favorite song. Buy yourself a flowering plant to improve your mood any time you see it or invite friends to an improvised party brunch to add some happy socialization to your life.

09. Practice neuroticism

It's not easy to live in a moment where the past yanks you backward, and the future scares the fuck out of you. Mindfulness, meditation, breathing exercises, and books awakening Your Life's Meaning will all help retrain an overactive brain.

10. Keep a notepad with you

Start and finish each day with a few lines and see what's coming out of it. There is a reasonable probability that you can suppress not only the noise but also obtain real insight into how you truly feel. It's also a perfect way to set a goal every morning and track success over time.

11. Verbalize your appreciation

Take the time every morning to say three things that you are grateful for, and then commit to letting everyone in your life know what you think about them every day. Gratitude makes people feel abundant and cheerful, making it much harder to be obsessive about what we don't have.

12. Help others

Maybe it's volunteering with an association or helping to watch a baby while a new mom gets a treatment. It could be as easy as asking a colleague if you could get a cup of coffee for them. The more we offer, the more we feel synchronized with the world.

13. Build a room that will sustain the life you desire

Have you ever found that when you walk in the sand on the beach, you get irritated in big crowds or more carefree and relaxed? It's an obvious fact that we're affected by our climate, which is good news for those of us who want to make a fresh start. A fresh coat of paint, a new piece of art, or a transformed bedroom or home office can be exactly what you need to get into a new mental zone.

14. Commit to being supportive of everyone

I can assure you that this is a difficult one (have you seen our taxi drivers or treated our visitors in the center of the city?). By committing yourself to kindness, you will develop an awareness of your normal emotions and begin to take actual control of your resources. Before you know it, you can be more forgiving about the latest (and slow) checkout clerk and see your stumbling blocks as part of the regular advancement of human growth.

15. Know that it doesn't have to be outstanding to be incredible

There's real strength in progress, and it's important to celebrate all the movement toward the goal. Any moment you want best for yourself is a victory, and while you might not be where you want to be, that doesn't mean you need to forget how far you've come.

The most popular ways to reclaim your life

If you're going to regain your life, you need to take some time to ask yourself a few questions. Do you live your life the way you want to live it? Can you find that you're going through your day as your real self? Are you speaking in your voice, or are you standing back out of fear of not being accepted? Avoid staying back so that you can rebuild your life. Many of us are struggling with the difference between whom we are and who we show to the public. We're doing this to get in. We fear that our loved ones or friends will criticize us for the things we do or the ways we wish to be. So instead of being ourselves, we waste so much energy striving to match what everyone else wants of us into this form.

1) Be your real self

Think seriously about who you were when you were a little girl. Haven't you been bold, tried new stuff, and done whatever you wanted? You were courageous in your pursuits, and it was beautiful. You've learned right from wrong things and teachings like don't place your hand on the burner, don't grab the dog's tail, and know how to share. When you mastered the fundamentals of life, you started to explore your identity and behave as your true self. Maybe you haven't blended in or have found yourself a bit "special," but that didn't discourage you. You became apolitical.

What's happening to any of us since then? Well, "Status" has occurred. Think about it, we say, and we do stuff depending on how others view us. Maybe you're no longer dreaming about the fantasy about what you want to do. You don't care about how you're going to do it because you're scared of failing someone or not working up to their expectations. Many successful individuals may be disturbing those around them, so they can stop at none to attain their aspirations of achievement. Those are the individuals who have established or learned a great deal of self-acceptance so that they can rebuild their lives. Don't hold back because you're scared of what people may say. Truly achieving success in life starts by believing that you are plenty and taking the same confidence from when you were a child to be your true self.

2) Try to limit the use of social media
They're all competing for your affection. In our social environments, whether formal or digital, we are being bombarded with emotions, suggestions, goods, services, etc. It can get stressful, and worse, we get

accustomed, and it goes unnoticed. Imagine wandering along the street for an hour. It's annoying for others. It's not walking; it's blinking signs, the pavement dancers, and the chaos. It's all competing for your time, and it may weigh on you. It is possible to make the same comparison for social media. Find the balance of the use of social media. I advise you to take note of what you are doing and where you are doing it (desktop computer, phone, mobile device).

3) Traveling

There's a wide world out there with new opportunities at every turn, and it's waiting for you to step out! Experience with individuals, places, and communities will give you to know experiences and the development of your own life. Travelling has a way to drive you out of your comfort zone, which carries with it a special kind of awareness to interact deeper with yourself and others. This is a perfect way to get you out there more and have a chat with fellow travelers or locals. You have become conscious of your schedule, your surroundings, and your general well-being. Most of us like to make arrangements when you're on the road, and if anything isn't for you, you'll adapt and move on. For some purpose, when we are in our hometowns, we can get complacent and remain in positions and circumstances that do not help us. Be a visitor in your area, do something new or more of the stuff you enjoy, visit a museum, go for a walk, look at architecture, go on a day trip, etc. I understand that there will be responsibilities and budgets to be followed. Take out unnecessary costs, set up a travel fund, and stick to it. It's either going to be "day one" or "one day."

4) Exercise daily

Exercise is beneficial not only emotionally but also psychologically. I still say nothing sounds better than a completed workout. The only thing is that you're going to have to endure the exercise. I prefer to go to community lessons led by a trainer, so I'm not the sort to go to a gym and know what to do to get the best results. Exercise will help you improve your life, and it's a perfect way to take time and take care of yourself, free your mind, and feel mentally and physically healthy. We prefer to reflect on what we've been working on all the time. However, we are not paying attention to our fellow human-being. If you don't seem to be committed, I suggest having a peer or workout partner to hold you honest. Or consider joining the exercise challenge so that you have a routine to execute and a target to strive for. When you know the best you can do, you can give the best to everyone and everything in life.

5) Have discussions take the day and chat thoroughly

There's something to tell about sitting across the table from your favorite person, having a cup of coffee, and enjoying a good chat. It's something I don't do nearly enough, but it's something I'm more able to do. While you're at it, make sure to ask questions and dig beyond the usual surface that conversations tend to be going on these days. Always speak honestly. And to enjoy the pleasures of love and friendships the way they were supposed to be.

6) Remove the waste that's irrelevant in your life

The old saying goes, "Where your trash is, there isn't your treasure." This begs an important question why do we end up with so much stuff that we don't end up using? Yeah, it's fair to say that all of us have excesses in our houses, in our cars, and our closets. Make the best of the items you don't need by donating or throwing it away. Let anyone else have and appreciate the things you don't have.

CHAPTER 5: THE THEORY OF THOUGHTS, FEELINGS, AND PERCEPTION

Certain things in life make people feel; they're called emotional responses. Some things in life make people wonder; often, they're called rational or analytical reactions. So, life is split between things that make you feel and think. The question is if anyone thinks, does that mean they're thinking less? Ah, it certainly does. If part of your brain is occupied with emotion, it makes sense for you to have less ability for thought. It's clear if you're taking emotional extremes, such as screaming, where people can hardly think at all. This doesn't mean that sensitive people aren't smart; it just means that they may be dumber at a time when they're exposed. Emotion goes on and on for everyone, sometimes people scream, and sometimes they're serious. Some things in life will, of course, induce more feeling than other things.

1. Black is more emotional than black and white. So, something likes that more color is going to be more expressive to look at, whether it's the contrast between a gold or silver sword and a gold or silver machine. In all cases, the gold would be more sentimental.

2. Things that are personal are emotional, unique things that people want and know are close to them. After all, it's a dentition of feeling, something that makes you feel. And if you like it, it's going to make you feel more. Other stuff, apart from the like, could trigger emotions, such as curiosity, but generally one of the stronger feelings. You might assume that the two are directly proportional; the more you like, the more you feel. Yet there are things people dream about like that. You might want something, and it's what makes you think, and we've previously rejected feeling as emotion, not thinking. Thoughts are apart from surfaces since belief is a phase of thinking. Think about the feelings; how did I feel about that? So, just a time of heightened emphasis is thought? Or is this a sudden increase in concentration based on one single thing that is clear? It's hard to

concentrate too much, though, if you feel a lot. This makes me believe that there is an overlap between sensing and thinking, like a Venn diagram. Yet there are still parts of thinking that there's no feeling or emotion in them, just parts of the emotion that they haven't considered. This means that thought takes more focus than a sense does, so we refused thought as a time of increased attention. You can be emotional and have more attention, but generally, if you're passionate, you'll be less attentive than you would be if you were thinking more. Again, whether you are emotional, you may be prudent to your feelings, whatever they may be, because if your feelings are like the light, then when you see the morning, you may be attentive to it so that you won't be worried about it.

Then you should pay attention to something and not care about it at the same time. Yet you're not going to pay attention to anything else. It appears, though, that thinking is more focused than a feeling. When you try to feel like your machine is always not as responsive as if you were worried about your device, again, that depends on what you're saying with your machine. If you think your machine sucks, you're going to pay it less focus than you think it's fantastic. It all depends on your thoughts about the machine. If you feel the device is acceptable, you'll pay more attention to it than if you think it's not good (possibly). Thoughts and emotions, however, correlate. That's if you think it's terrible, then you're going to believe it's awful. So, thinking and emotion are the same things. Yet the ideas are much stronger than the feelings. Thinking and feeling should offer the same amount of attention to something, but the review is more precise. It's more accurate for you to believe that your computer is okay than to feel that your computer is okay. Who knows why you believe the machine is fine because if you thought the engine was fair, you'd understand why you felt it was? Emotions and emotions are more mysterious.

So, the better you like something (or dislike something), Emotional responses to something, the more emotional they are, but they're not mean it might not allow you to worry about it, either. However, one cannot mark anything in life as either feeling or thought. Life is not a scale of feeling on one end and thinking on the other. There are also causes present, such as dopamine and physical activity, which can also trigger heightened concentration that is not either emotional or thoughtful. When you're running, you've got a lot of focus on the fact that you're running, and you're not worrying about it or getting emotional about it. This means that just because you like something, it doesn't mean it's sentimental. You might want to race, but it doesn't make you feel emotions. So, what does sentiment mean? Emotions should be thoughts that you can't define because when you think something, it must be that you're unconsciously thinking about that. You just don't know what it is, usually. Thoughts and feelings are emotions. By that, I mean, they can be broken down into pieces, and they can be ensured what those parts are. And the thoughts are all actual pieces that you can recognize. So, the distinction between emotions, feelings, and perceptions is that you know what your perceptions are about it. Still, you don't have as clear an understanding of what emotions and feelings are, as they are more obscure and more difficult to define. So, if you know what triggers the surface, it's no longer a feeling, but it's a thought (i.e., so you call the emotion a review because the idea is always producing emotion.

Some behavior interpretation points

There are two kinds of observations in the theory of emotions; one category is everyday general observations (such as sex is good for someone's mental health). And the other type is practical observations (when one's emotion ceases for a second and the other takes its place, what's going on there, what's going on there, why do they stop and resume, etc.

- Emotions stop and resume all the time. This stopping and beginning could happen as rapid changes or smooth transitions, one feeling eventually fading into the other. However, this is not a complete description of how emotion works. Humans are likely to have a variety of emotions happening at one time, each of which communicates with one or more other emotions and potentially triggers them to cease, resume, fade, or increase.

- Feelings such as anger, affection, traumatic feelings, sexual emotions, positive emotions, and amusing emotions are all likely to connect and to be felt to a degree all the time. These are only a couple of emotions/feelings that are probably felt a lot every day.

- There are noticeable phenomena that exist with certain feelings, such as happiness will relieve discomfort and make a painful feeling go away.

- Life is intense and constant, so intense feeling is likely to be sustained in humans all the time. These feelings might stop and continue, someone might go from short bursts of stress to low-intensity outbreaks, but the point is that the pressure is felt, and the constant flow of emotional development is continuous.

- There are also emotional states that can change your view on life or how you would react to a situation. Fear, rage, compassion, and admiration are all emotional states that affect the way you respond to incidents. You can also be in a condition of preparation for such feelings, be prepared to feel pain or joy, or be in one of those states.

- Emotions are perceived consciously and implicitly; the extent to which someone experiences explicit sentiment is the degree to which they are aware. When a feeling is perceived but is not within the consciousness of the person who is feeling it, ignorance is often an unconscious emotion, so they are not aware of it. Someone may feel a great deal of emotion, but that doesn't mean that the feeling is going to be entirely under the consciousness of the person who is feeling it. They may be explaining the emotion as feeling like it's high, but they may not be in contact with it (making it more unconscious). It is in this world of "apparently greater feelings" that emotional development takes place. Unconsciously, there are far more feelings you experience than you are truly aware of them. It is there, therefore, in the unconscious mind that emotions interact in great detail and intensity, barely being consciously sensed at times, and with the person perhaps only keenly aware that something emotional may be going on (unconsciously).

- Any person perceives emotion. Emotion evokes a specific emotional reaction in a person. That person is who they are, but we all inhabit the same universe. There would be critical psychological items in that person that are commonly perceived to be necessary to other people, such as death or marriage. Every person has peculiarities and particulars on what would cause a big emotional reaction. It wouldn't always be something that they "like a lot," but more things that they consciously or unconsciously are supposed to be.

- When emotion may stop and continue, and there could be phases of intensity and low intensity, one asks how many of the different emotional states there are. It's a mental state with any mood in a social circumstance you might tell. If a particular perspective is present, then people will feel certain things and react in a way that corresponds to that mood. But it's just social moods. There are several different ways people's emotional state will change; whether you're working on something that you like working on, you may be in a particular emotional state for that.

- An emotional state includes a particular collection of emotions that result from a specific occurrence or in certain conditions.

- An important observation to remember in the theory of emotions is that pain will interrupt the immediate flow of emotion or feeling and notify the individual. Pain and fear derive from other surfaces because they are harmful. How much do feelings like hope or fun get distorted by the feelings of discomfort? Is it a fun feeling, or is it an emotional state? Happy will mean that you are undergoing a series of textures that make that situation happy, that joy is emotion, that "fun" is more of a mental state.

- The rhythm of someone's feelings will disappear all of a sudden, suggest you're sleeping in bed after you wake up, then your alarm clock goes off- you've gone from having content, peaceful emotions to those that unexpectedly end up. Feelings and thoughts pause and resume like that all the time. In a talk, for example, someone could be happy, and the other person could show a depressed expression, and it could immediately bring an end to other people's happiness. There are many feelings that someone might take in a conversation, such as shyness or an emotion voicing a thought or an opinion, and these feelings might affect (or start and stop) the feelings that the other person is feeling. It should be clear that the multiple sensations that someone feels during the day change all the time, breaks, begins, shifts, and changes in complex ways all the time.

- Emotion will inspire the mind. People are going to different states or 'modes' where they are motivated to think about a particular form of thinking or to do some action. When someone enters another country, such as a pleasure-seeking state, the model is driven, in turn, by emotion. It's apparent that everyone is feeling more joy, so you'd say it's caused by desire. However, any state that someone is in, any slight, every slight social, mental state, or mental state that someone is doing a job is going to have some emotion or feeling behind it. But it's not just a compilation of emotions, the experience is outstanding every time, and this individuality communicates some knowledge that is also special. Feeling shows you what you want and what you don't like; it's probably the main feelings (pleasure and pain). But each other's emotion expresses something-if you feel guilty, you know what that feeling means; maybe that feeling in conjunction with other emotions represents something dead or unique, depending on the collection of emotions that it is and what it means in that sense.

- As a consequence, someone may enter a mode such as violence, where they are emotionally abusive. It makes sense that, because this is a mode, it takes a fair amount of time to experience it. It's not a word or a gesture that takes a few seconds, but a method like this, I imagine, will take at least a couple of minutes. Another mode may be comedic. Perhaps it's evident to the person being watched as entertained-but possibly internally, and they're entertained for a certain amount of time before and during the observation that they're that way.

- It's not to suggest that for a few seconds, anyone couldn't have had entertained feelings. When someone smiles, the emotions usually last only for the duration of amusement. Yet they may also have been considered for a while afterward. You laughed- and after that. You'll be satisfied or entertained. My point about modes is that there are some strong sets of feelings that linger for a while-like joy of looking for a collection of feelings. That's the product of laughter or humor; this is a deep, particular mode that gives a group of feelings to someone. Maybe anyone else has a different mode-maybe. They have a powerful method where they feel bad, and they have a particular collection of emotions and opinions in this mode.

Thoughts

What's the difference between thought, sensation, perception, reasoning, and intelligence? It needs a lot of attention to use all of them. And when you're in, there's something emotional that your mind is drawn to that thing. The reason is that anything in life will inevitably result in a sensation. Even emotion is the product of thought. The feeling is the unconscious thinking of things, and the idea is the conscious thought of something. Thought results in emotions, but unconscious thinking (emotion) would also result in feelings. If you think of it that way, thinking and sentiment are both part-feelings, that is, to the degree you feel them right now, as well as handling them later. But it always means the emotion is still the end product. Again, ideas can be the product of current thoughts. It's like emotion; involuntary emotional thinking can later lead to implicit emotional thinking. Even emotions could be considered unconscious thinking because opinion only focuses on one thing for a short amount of time. So sentiment, thought, and sensation is all cycles of concentration on those things. With thinking, you remember what it's like you're concentrating on it. With feelings, you care enormously about what you're focused on, and you care less about it. Physical stimulation often causes emotions, and then you concentrate on those emotions, but you don't focus on what triggered the feelings (physical stimulation itself).

So, life is just the kind of feeling you have; you might categories all life as feeling. And when you think you're in a time when you don't feel anything, you feel something; you just don't know what you're feeling. Know the emotions are ideas that you can't identify. The dentition of intelligence and thought is nearly comprehension (those concrete things). The feeling is emotion, totally different from facts or knowledge. Both the points and experience will be about things that make you feel, though, because all the things that happen lead you to handle, because all the facts and information is about things that happen. Intellect and thinking often give rise to emotions as specific ideas are stored in your head. Since thought is just about feelings, it is evident that thinking is rooted in emotions. E.g., all processes are just emotions in mind, so the mind is only contrasting emotions. You're taking two feelings, and you should come up with one idea. Take the sensation of a frog swimming and a sense of danger. The two emotions together are equal to the notion or perception that the frog wants to travel when there is a risk that the perception is simply only knowing how emotions communicate. All thinking is to consider how emotions and actual situations communicate with themselves. The feeling is what gives the drive to come to the solution (the thought). If you've just got the truth, there's a threat, and the frog will leap, you're not going to conclude that the frog can jump away. You need to sense like there are a danger and sense that the frog will leap and then merge the two visual images in your mind to get the answer.

This shows how a complete mind is powered and motivated by emotion. It also indicates that the frogs have thoughts; the frog needs to have the idea to run away when it sees danger, as the concept is only a mixture of two emotions, resulting in a feeling of having to run forward. This method of sense is like a process of thinking. Thoughts are a bit different for humans; however, since humans have such a large memory that they can equate this experience with the other experiences of their lives. At the same time, the frog only remembers the present situation and is conditioned to jump away (brain wiring). The frog doesn't have enough memory to learn about new knowledge and alter its actions. This illustrates how humans are somewhat similar to frogs in the manner they process.

Feelings and thoughts and the way to alter them

Emotion is more like a mental feeling than conscious thought. While sentiment and texture can be described as unconscious thinking, one of is going to be more like conscious thinking. Emotions are just like impulses when you touch what you're feeling. Therefore, sensations are easier than motivations and perceptions because when you connect something, there is a small pause until you can think about it (thought) or feel something strongly about it (emotion). Emotion is thus an unconscious feeling. It can also be best described as a cold feeling (so that sensation is like a conscious emotion. You can feel it more robust and faster, but the sentiment is a more profound, more implicit sensation comparable to inferential thinking. But feelings are often more similar to conscious thought, so thinking is a profound experience when the sense is strong or superficial but not deep). One definition of emotion may be "any intense feeling." Many conclusions can be taken from this definition. Simple (or primary) emotions can be made up of secondary emotions such as passion can include feelings or emotions of envy, desire, and longing. Feelings may be explained in greater depth than emotions, and you may have a particular sense about something, every surface is new, and you do not have a title. For example, if you're annoyed by a person who may have a feeling of his own because that person upsets you in a certain way. The surface doesn't have a negated name, so it's your unique feeling. The feeling may also be an emotion.

"Distress" is too weak to be an emotion, but it doesn't mean it's not as intense as feelings are intense in other respects. Unemotional is just a feeling, though. There is complete overlap in how emotions feel and how feelings feel, which is identical. So, there are only a few defined feelings, but there is an unlimited number of ways to experience things. You might have a "weak" sense of hatred. Then you may say that you have a sense of hatred then, whether it's big, you might claim that you're emotional about hatred, or that you're feeling a sense of disgust. You can have the same hate feeling in different circumstances, but every time you think you're going to be at least significantly different. You should remember some emotion; that's what makes it feel. If you're down, that's a feeling, but if you're depressed, that's not a feeling; it's just like an impulse. You can't work out why you're depressed, but you can usually point out why you're unhappy. Feelings are more realistic, and whether anything occurs or happens, it will give rise to an emotion. It's otherwise known as feeling. So, emotions are unconscious impulses, which are the product of unconscious thoughts—feeling defined as someone you could recognize. So, you can't identify the unconscious mind that triggered the cold feeling, but you can describe the involuntary feeling.

Experiential practitioners see the cognitive processing of clients as happening on a continuum of five stages

    i. Pre-reflective response to emotional stimuli, which includes awareness of stimuli, pre-conscious emotional and cognitive processing, and associated physiological changes

    ii. Knowledge and understanding of the reaction

    iii. Labeling and understanding of the behavioral responses, using internal as well as situational cues to classify their reactions.

iv. Evaluation of whether or not the answer is appropriate.

Cognitive-behavioral therapy (CBT)

Cognitive Behavioral Therapy is a type of psychotherapy that looks at each other.

1) What do you think of yourself, the community, and other people?

2) How it affects you and how it affects your emotions and feelings.

CBT will make you learn and start to improve some of the ways you say and do. Having improvements will make people feel better for them.

CBT and health appearance

CBT was first explicitly used for conditions such as anxiety and bad mood, specifically influencing people's behavioral and emotional well-being. There is growing evidence that it is beneficial across a wide variety of conditions like CFS / ME and other medical conditions such as Irritable Bowel Syndrome (IBS), Multiple Sclerosis (MS), arthritis, and Chronic Pain. This does not mean that all disorders are considered to be neurological or that people's physical symptoms are not being treated seriously. It does appear, though, that the way we cope with illness in terms of our emotional responses, our feelings about ourselves and our futures, and the way we respond will make a significant difference in how much illness affects us. Using a CBT approach is not attempting to reduce the problem by calling it "psychological." It is merely about trying to interpret the issue holistically, looking at how the condition influences and affects aspects like sleep habits. Your interactions, your way of dealing with stress, your diet, your attitudes, your activity style (laid back, motivated, etc.) as well as the way you think about it.

A cognitive-Behavioral model of the CFS/ME

The cognitive-behavioral model of CFS/ME explores relevant factors that may have been present before CFS / ME (predisposing factors). It also looks at the causes that were present at the onset of the disease (precipitating reasons) and those that could sustain the illness and make it more difficult to progress towards healing (retaining factors).

Factors contributing

There is an indication that the following can increase vulnerability to CFS / ME. Some people may consider all of them as necessary, while others may find like none of them applies in their situation. There aren't one size fits all strategy.

1. Ever disturbing sleep habits.

2. The childhood trauma.

3. Genetic susceptibility – this is unproven, although groups of individuals in certain families have demonstrated that there might be a genetic propensity to be vulnerable to the disease.

4. Personality People with CFS / ME also describe being hard-working, attentive, and have high expectations of themselves. This style of personality can contribute to individuals working very hard to accomplish whatever they do, leaving little time for fun.

5. Very busy/healthy lifestyle and no rest.

Precipitation factors

You will be able to classify any, but certainly not all, of the triggers mentioned below.

1. Infection

Viral infection, such as glandular fever, is commonly identified as the starting point for CFS / ME. Often people mention developing several illnesses. However, there is no strong indication that the virus or bacteria can remain after CFS / ME has been identified, even if you might still believe that you have an infection from which you have not fully healed.

2. Lifestyles

Fatigue can grow and become chronic in combination with an overcrowded lifestyle and little time for rest. This is most likely to be associated with CFS / ME when, after illness/infection, a person feels under strain to reach their previous degree of dedication before being thoroughly recovered.

3. Events in life

Substantial life changes, such as changing jobs, getting married, maternity, moving home, a relapse, leaving a long-term relationship, can all be traumatic occurrences that can contribute to increased susceptibility to CFS / ME.

4. There is no apparent reason

Any individuals would report that their illness evolved for no evident cause that "out of the blue" seemed to arrive.

Maintenance of Influences

Just as there are many factors involved with the growth of CFS/ME, there are many factors that can support it. For example,

1. Doing more rest

While resting for a short period is the best thing to do when you have a severe illness or infection, extended rest will delay healing and cause a variety of problems. Some data indicate that extended rest after a viral disease could increase the severity of fatigue six months later. Extended rest can decrease activity resistance and affect other body systems.

2. The trend of boom and bust activity

Over-vigorous activity or exercise that alternates with resting for long periods to heal can unintentionally make the issue worse in the longer term since it is challenging to develop a regular pattern.

3. Receive conflicting notifications on controlling your health

Receiving multiple messages from experts as well as family and friends may have prompted you to feel confused about what to do for the better and pursue several methods that have not been effective.

4. Disturbed sleep habits

Irregular sleep-time, waking up, or resting or sleeping too long throughout the day, can lead to a disrupted and refreshing night's sleep. It has a direct effect on exhaustion and other symptoms.

5. Life stress and low moods

Some individuals with CFS / ME experience significant life-long stress and disease-related complications. They will include: -

- Economic difficulties
- Care about the maintenance of jobs, the maintenance of research, etc.
- A shift in the position of the family, e.g., lack of duty
- Decreased social interactions contributing to feelings of isolation
- Feeling wrong about not being a "successful" parent

These problems will understandably cause feelings of anger, helplessness, and lack of control over life. These are all the emotions that are a normal stress reaction that can lead to depression or anxiety disorders for some people. Depression may intensify weakness and further reduce the incentive to be involved. Excessive fear may be a further drain of limited energy.

6. Major cause focusing on

It is understandable to think about recurring symptoms. Unfortunately, the downside to this is that often concentrating on symptoms makes them more daunting.

7. Worries over the condition that causes the disease worse

Often, during an operation, people perceive increased discomfort or exhaustion as an indication of damage to the body. This can lead to an overemphasis on the rest period.

Behavioral therapy approach to handling CFS/ME

This method is designed to help you find the most useful ways to treat your disease. This would include assisting you in making improvements to any trends that could be partly responsible for preserving your

CFS/ME. It also seeks to help you develop techniques to cope with other factors-physical, mental, or social-that can impair your condition.

This will include: -

1. Checking your level of activity

By completing a task log at least once, you can get an accurate view of what you do every day and where you will need to make improvements.

2. Setting the goals

To help you concentrate on what you'd like to do in the next few months.

3. Stabilizing your action and your rest

It would be necessary to add brief bursts of true relaxation if you usually do too much.

4. Increase or change your routines

If you have developed a schedule that involves scheduled action and rest, you will take measures to move towards your goals. This would include a somewhat incremental improvement in such tasks, such as fitness and cognitive activities, the potential implementation of new rewarding behaviors, and, in some instances, a decrease in activities such as long working hours.

5. Establishing a sleeping schedule

How you do this depends on the issue of sleep you might have. It could include cutting rest during the day, reducing sleep at night, and waking up and going to bed regularly.

6. Learning how to tackle unhelpful feelings and attitudes

This will initially include finding thoughts that can impede your success and result in you becoming discouraged, such as "I'm never going to get any better" or "I haven't done anything today." Then you will learn to question these ideas by coming up with more useful alternatives.

7. Learn how to maintain your gains and make further progress

It would include a more in-depth view of your condition, such as the causes that sustain or worsen it, learning ways to fix these problem areas, and how to continue moving towards your long-term goals. Besides, you can learn how to deal with future challenges that will make continuing development complicated.

Negative thought and emotions

At times, we all have pessimistic feelings, even without knowing. This is because Automatic Pessimistic Thinking, like Insects, can be challenging to detect. They're 'Automatic,' and they appear to jump into the mind without any cognitive control. They also seem rational and real, and they are too cynical and twisted when they take a closer look. Negative emotions are harmful and pointless. They can lead to destructive thoughts and acts, and they can place a lot of added pressure on you.

Negative thoughts can inhibit a practical approach

Wrong thought can lead to a vicious circle. It prevents you from having control and sometimes ends up making you feel bad. An idea might be like a droplet of water, causing a wave in a still pool. Similarly, pessimistic (and optimistic) emotions may have a ripple effect.

Resolving roadblocks – ANTS management

Learning to understand Automatic Negative Thinking is the first step toward interrupting the negative 'think-feeling-behavior loop. Once you know your ANTS for what they are, you just don't believe it's real. You should question them, too. This is going to help you come up with a more practical and helpful solution.

There are a variety of popular 'distorted perception' loops. Are you going to stumble into all of them?

Catastrophizing – Thinking the worse is always likely to happen in a case like this. You find it challenging. Often people think that if something goes wrong,

Disaster is expected to happen. For example, if the day begins terribly, Involuntary Pessimistic Thinking (ANTS) might be that it will only get worse.

Overgeneralization – this is why we treat one mistake or loss as proof of a general rule as to how bad things are. E.g., if one day you quit ironing because of your symptoms, you could find yourself thinking, "I'm never going to be able to do it."

Black and white thinking – Are you thinking about it now or nothing? Almost it's all relative. An example of black and white reasoning would have been to say that once you do it all right, you're a loser. It's not easy to do everything right all the time. People will also set unrealistically high expectations for them and blame themselves for doing so. They're making even minor mistakes. Know that there are usually shades of grey.

Double standards – Assuming that other people can make errors or slips people, but not on your own. It could be useful to ask yourself why you need to

Well, be too subtle.

Amplification – This happens as we exaggerate the severity of our challenges or deficiencies and underestimate the significance of our strengths.

Cognitive filters – This happens when we pick up single negative information. Just remain on it solely. This can cloud our view of reality. For instance, we may get a lot of encouraging feedback from our families, but if one of them says something slightly critical, we may hang on their words for days and forget some of the constructive reviews.

Disregarding the positive – This happens when we dismiss festive events by insisting that they do not count. When you reach a target, you can convince yourself that it wasn't good enough or that someone should do it. This will strip the fun out of your life and make you feel inadequate and unrewarded.

Jumping to conclusions – This happens when people get pessimistic Conclusions about items in the absence of any clear evidence. Often this sort of thing is called mind-reading, without testing the evidence why you conclude someone's mind-reading. It's responding emotionally to you. You could have someone muttering and assume its self-criticism; maybe they're just trying to recall their shopping list.

Fortune telling – You guess something may turn out to be wrong and will cease you from even trying it out.

Complete assumptions – When people say words that should or should never be used, they also feel elevated levels of remorse, fear, and anger. People also have such thoughts when they want to abide by personal laws and expectations that could be too strict and too difficult. These living rules are also complicated to achieve and possibly have very little practical relevance to daily life (e.g., I must always look at my best, or people won't like me).

Emotional thinking – This happens when we focus our opinion on the way we feel at the moment (rather than standing back and thinking it up).

CHAPTER 6: WAYS TO CONTROL THOUGHTS

Thoughts may be our worst partners and our worst rivals. Everyone has had a moment where their brain has a brain of its own, so having care of your emotions will make you happy, less anxious, and more prepared to fix issues or accomplish goals. Read on for more tips on how to regain care of your brain. Negative feelings can be about us, about others, about our circumstances, about the world in general, about the past, about the future. People often get into the habit of thinking negatively if they're living with them. Our awareness is considered in three sections: behavior, feelings, and thoughts.

- Depression and anxiety
- Distress
- Low self-esteem
- Personality-hatred

Situations and other people's treatment of us can evoke and intensify these emotional states, but we also reinforce them if we neglect to recognize our patterns of negative thought and fail to question these patterns. These three components are intricately linked. Thus, pessimistic thoughts will lead to destructive emotions and unconstructive behavior. E.g., if you always say, "I'm worthless," you're apt to fall into a depressive mood and isolate from people. So they don't see how useless you are.

When you are alone, frustrated, and unhappy, you are more likely to think negatively. Your attitude influences your feelings, and your loneliness means that you are not with any people who may explicitly or implicitly challenge your view of yourself. So, you can be caught in a vicious cycle. Banishing pessimistic feelings, through practice, will lead to positive moods, improved self-confidence, more positive ways of living, and healthier relationships. There are two steps to remove destructive emotions: Recognize them and CHALLENGING them to your mind.

Negative thought Identification

There are a variety of prevalent patterns of negative thought. Take one of your usual depressive feelings and see if it suits one or more of the following trends.

1. All or Nothing Thought doesn't leave any middle ground – if anything doesn't go, it was utterly "an absolute disaster." You're "ugly" if you don't dress like a model.

2. If the presentation wasn't "excellent," it was "ruby." You can also use terms inside your mind as you say, like, "always, sometimes, nobody, all the time," etc.

3. Overgeneralizing exaggerates the relevant details; if two females in a row end up with you, you say to yourself, "Women always leave me in the end." It can lead to classification as a result–whether you have backed out of a couple of romantic scenarios and then mark yourself as "female/male doomed" or "absolute coward." Labels don't make us feel optimistic about ourselves or the

243

prospect of change. Mental Screening is confronted with a vast amount of information but homing in only on the bad aspects of it and forgets the rest of it. So maybe you'll be composing your CV and winding up discouraged because you're worried about the loss of job experience or your A-level scores.

4. Discounting Optimistic is close to that of behavioral filtering.

   a) You recognize or acknowledge your positive attributes or achievements, but you will not count them or mark them as significant.

   b) It was such a fluke with that assignment.

   c) Look good today, but they say it to cheer me up.

   d) You're not even conscious of your good attributes or accomplishments.

5. The Crystal Ball, or "Fortune Prediction," is referring to you as if you had the right to know what the future holds if you don't! "I will never discover, "If I go to their house party, I'm going to feel like I'm out of it." This is projecting negative memories and perceptions from the present and past forward as though they will necessarily linger with you or be replicated. You might also create a picture of a potential occurrence in your mind and then assume that the image is an accurate reflection of what's going to happen "for sure."

6. Mind reading is thinking that you know what other people are or are going to think, even if they haven't said something or they're not there. "They think I'm lazy," "they think I should have come back with her," or "he'll

think I'm very sorry if I ask him to help me."

7. Emotional thinking is when you consider your destructive emotions as proof of the facts/truths about yourself or your circumstance. "I feel terrible, so I must have done the wrong thing" or "I feel so negative, I must be a bad guy." It can also contribute to labels such as "I'm still sad; I must be a stressed guy."

8. 8. Personalization (sometimes referred to as a misallocation) is where you mentally take it.

9. Responsibility for something that was not, or is not your responsibility. "It's my mistake that he was so bad to me at that lecture; I was supposed to keep quiet;" "It's my fault that Mum was so sick; I was supposed to be out and sit at home for a year."

These three components are intricately linked. Thus, pessimistic thoughts will lead to destructive emotions and unconstructive behavior. E.g., if you always say, "I'm worthless," you're apt to fall into a depressive mood and isolate from people. So they don't see how useless you are. When you are alone, frustrated, and unhappy, you are more likely to think negatively. Your attitude influences your feelings, and your loneliness means that you are not with any people who may explicitly or implicitly challenge your view of yourself. So, you can be caught in a vicious cycle. Banishing pessimistic feelings, through practice, will lead to positive moods, improved self-confidence, more positive ways of living, and healthier relationships. There are two steps to remove destructive emotions: Recognize them and CHALLENGING them to your mind.

Poor, challenging thinking

You challenge your thinking by challenging how valid/genuine/rational it is, and there are various ways of questioning that can be used individually or in combination.

1. Do I have enough details to come to that conclusion? Is there any apparent difference in my knowledge of the facts? If I had learned more, it would have been possible to think, Is there anything different? If so, stop thinking negatively and get the facts.

2. What justification is there to support this idea? And what is the proof against it? In the context of all the facts, I have accomplished a reasonable and balanced point of view? If not, what would be a fair and equitable, more accurate way of thinking?

248

3. (For fears of something negative going on in the future) what is realistic? Am I underestimating my chances because of my fear? What other possible outcomes are there? Have I underestimated my own ability to deal with a potential difficulty?

4. Am I in the habit of worrying about this? How did I learn about this habit? Am I trying to repeat the put-downs that someone/others in my history offer me? In their appraisal of me, were they honest and fair? Will my closest friend be following my thinking? Should I have been less critical about this scenario if it was a person who was in it rather than me? Do I have a norm for other people and myself? Do I want myself to be perfect? If I do, I set myself up for a good or sad existence?

5. Answering a "What if?" "The concerns you pose if you can answer "What if," then you can create a variety of choices that can help you reduce your anxiety.

Release pessimistic feelings

If you have analyzed and questioned your views as mentioned, you will be able to replace them with more constructive, or at the very least, more logical and objective thoughts. As well as the emotional relief of this, it is highly likely that speaking more favorably about yourself and your condition will improve your attitude and your self-esteem over time. Challenging the pessimistic emotions and replacing them with positive ones is a process that needs to be mastered and exercised like any other. Could you not give it up? Over time, you'll get stronger and better to capture your self-critical, fearful, negative feelings, and to assess, question, and alter them more easily.

Take care of your emotions

Stop it, and take a deep breath. Pause the out-of-control line of thought, merely thinking, "Wait," Take a few deep breaths to compose yourself before you move on, helping you to answer your feelings only and with a level mind. By concentrating your attention on your breathing for a second, you can remove yourself from your emotions and make them easier to control. Studies suggest that it takes 90 seconds for neurochemical stimuli to fade out from the brain and revert to standard brain chemistry, so try counting to 90 seconds to stay calm.

Stay in Present

Continually ruminating on the past that you cannot alter, or dreaming into the future that you cannot anticipate. It is a sure way to lose control of your emotions. Rely on the here and now, the most actual condition in which you can manage, and your feelings can follow. Practice a quick grounding technique like sitting in a chair, concentrating on what the feet feel like as they hit the surface. This will help you relate to what you're doing at the moment and adjust to other issues. Many spiritual traditions suggest remaining at the moment to cultivate inner harmony and clarity. An easy question to ask yourself is: what can I do to change the way I feel right now?

Observe your feelings with no judgment

After a pause, go back to your feelings without blaming yourself for making them. Remember that you had those feelings and what made you feel like you've lost control of your brain. Having an analytical look at your feelings will help you make sense of them without generating destructive emotions. Keep to concrete, factual truth. If you're in a fight, don't accuse or speculate whether the other side is crazy. Consider what the circumstances led to the war, what can be done to bring an end to it, and what made you furious. Instead of "I'm so bad with people, it's my fault that I don't have a girlfriend," say, "I haven't found love yet because I haven't met anyone who's so compatible with me." If you're having problems, write down your feelings and read them back to yourself.

Take steps to get your ideas straight

Sitting with your thoughts without intervention leads to an infinite loop of thinking. Make a strategy to resolve your thoughts and fears, as confusion is always at the center of rogue thoughts. If you can't stop worrying about jobs, for example, prepare to isolate your work life from your home life by taking time off, working less from home, or pursuing a new career that you love.

- Often, we can't control our emotions, and we're afraid to move on them.
- If you've made these arrangements, you need to see them through.
- If your emotions are skewed, or you feel continually out of balance, you will wish to pursue self-help or clinical counseling.

Place yourself in a comfortable atmosphere

The outer world profoundly influences the inner world because whether you are in an atmosphere where you feel insecure or out of control, the emotions will represent those feelings. Put on music that will calm you, light a candle, or go to your favorite place.

- Fragrances like tea tree, chamomile, and scented candles have been known to calm you and can help you control your thoughts.

- Try to take a stroll out of nature. Green space is known to relax your mind, mainly if you live in an urban environment. Find a park, beach, or hiking trail and take some time to get off the ground.

Temporarily, distract your thoughts with another task

Go for a stroll, watch a movie, or call a friend to get your mind off the thoughts at hand. Do something that you can do right away, and that doesn't cause you to hang around anymore with your crooked feelings.

- If, for example, you stand in line or feel out of reach in a traffic jam, occupy yourself by attempting to count down from 100 to 7s.
- Take note of the things that will help you rest and focus on your weekly schedule.
- However, note that this is a short-term approach. You should also be working on how to contain your emotions when you cannot "hide" them.

Speak to somebody to keep your feelings out of the open

Getting a new outlook on your mind will always clear you away in minutes, and expressing your emotions stops you from hearing it in your head over and over again.

- Good people are to share with our mates, parents, and professional counselors.

- If you're uncomfortable, start by saying, "I've got something to get out of my chest," or, "I've had something on my mind all day, would you mind listening for a while?"

Don't attempt to pick your emotions, but monitor them as they arrive

The human brain is an extraordinary organ capable of making creative strides, remembering memories, and seeking ideas at a moment's notice, and you can never control every thought. Learn to watch your emotions come and go without attachment, rather than repress any you don't wish to have.

- Thinking about ignoring something, paradoxically, it never succeeds. Any time you dream of not worrying about anything, you're thinking about it, of course.

Make your emotions and your psychological health a priority

- Take care of your brain by sleeping 7-8 hours a night, controlling your stress levels, and maintaining a positive outlook on life.
- Consuming and exercising nutritious meals often encourages improved mental and physical health.

Know what events are triggering difficult thoughts

While you're not supposed to avoid all of your problems, be aware of things that move your thoughts in a negative direction, and prepare yourself when they arise. Structure your day in such a way that you end up with a positive trigger, such as creative work, family time, or a good book, allowing you to spend time off thinking about the things you love.

- Take a few minutes a day to pause and stay aware of your life.
- Be mindful of your emotions at "trigger times," again forgoing judgment or self-criticism.

Relax

Throughout the years, meditation has become a vital method to help people calm and regain hold of their emotions. Meditation has also been shown to contribute to a healthier body and heart.

Reframe your reflections in a constructive or non-intrusive light

Reframing your feelings places them in the background of the world around you, helping you to understand them better. Remember other views on the case, as well as the actions of others. Work to cultivate empathy since this will help you stop taking something too literally. For instance, if someone you love hasn't called in a while, it's because they're busy or depressed, not sick or in danger.

Learn that there are a lot of things you can't manage

Don't be obsessive about something that you can't affect other people, the weather, the media, and just focus on yourself. When you worry about something beyond your influence, note that the only one you can influence is yourself, and focus on that. This does not mean that you do not aspire to make an effect on the world around you, but that you will still have the best impact on your feelings.

Practical strategies for overcoming negative feelings (and support optimistic thinking)

The dissatisfaction that emerges from inside of you or in the world around you will quickly become poisonous and prevent you from enjoying the life you want.

Find out what's better when you're in what feels like a tricky situation

If you have had a failure, slipped, or lost so that things could look daunting and pessimistic feelings could tend to emerge and threaten to fill your vision of this situation. To counteract this by asking yourself better questions.

Things like:

- What's a positive thing in this situation?
- What is one thing I should do differently the next time to get a better result?
- What kind of thing can I learn from this?
- How can my best friend motivate me in this circumstance?

Remember: people don't necessarily care about what you think or do

It's easy to get stuck into pessimistic feelings when you worry about what people might say or think if you do or don't do something. And then you're zapping your control, and maybe you're caught in analysis paralysis. Getting trapped in your mind and those thoughts can pull you farther away from what you want and from reality. And the fact is, people, don't have too much time, focus, or patience to think or talk about what you're doing. They have their hands and brains filled with children, careers, pets, interests, and their worries and concerns (like, for example, what people would think of them). This realization and a reminder will help you set yourself free from the limitations that you can build in your head and help you start taking small or more significant steps for what you desire deep down in your life.

Replace the uncertainty of your environment

What you let in your head in your day-to-day life would have a significant influence on you. Then start wondering what you're letting in. Ask yourself these questions: What are the top three causes of negativity in my life? They could be people, websites, magazines, newsletters, music, and so on. Then ask yourself: What will I do to waste less time with these three outlets in the week? If you can't find opportunities to do it right now with all three of them, take the small measure and work on doing it for only one of these outlets. Then use the time that you've freed up this week on more meaningful outlets and things that are either in your life or who you want to explore and maybe make a different part of it.

Stop getting the peaks of molehills

To avoid a little negative thought from being a massive brute in your head, face it early. You may do this by, for example, using the above tip. And maybe you should zoom out. Do this by posing yourself a question like this: Is this going to matter in 5 years? Or maybe this is going for five weeks? In most situations, this solution is not going to happen, and you were only starting to make a mountain out of a molehill (or out of thin air).

Let it go out and talk about it

Holding unpleasant feelings that start clouding your entire mind locked up won't help. But please let them out. Speak to someone close to you about the situation or your feelings. Only venting for a few minutes will also help you see the problem differently. Or, if not, then a discussion about it, where the two of you have a more valuable viewpoint and even the beginnings of an action plan, will be both relieving and refueling.

Stay in and go back to this point

Once you hit depressive thoughts, you're always thoughts about something that's happened or something that could occur. Or all of them, they all jumbled as your attitude and your emotions go down. Put your mind to this moment instead of snapping it out. Learn to make it a habit to devote all of your time to the current moment. You would naturally have fewer pessimistic feelings and be more open and positive. There are a few approaches to get you back to mindfulness, and this moment is:

- **Concentrate on breathing only**

Take a 1-2-minute rest right now and breathe a bit slower than you usually do. Ensure you're breathing from your stomach and nose. Only concentrate on the air coming in and out and nothing else at this moment.

- **Bring the world surrounding you**

Take 1-2-minute rest, get out of your mind, and pay attention to what's going on around you right now. Only concentrate on the people passing outside your window, the muffled voices and sounds of the street, the senses around you, and the sun shines in and warms your face.

Go for a little exercise

Go for a 20-30-minute exercise and lift light weights. This is going to help you free up inner tension and worry. And once again, it will make the mind concentrated and productive.

Don't let your ambiguous doubts bring you down

One fundamental mistake people make when it comes to fear to get scared and run away from them instead of looking more closely. It's natural to have the urge, of course, and to try to stop it, but when fears are ambiguous, they can become too much more disturbing than they need. Realistically, what's the worst thing that could happen in this scenario? When you try to ground your fear like that and start staring at it with your feet firmly rooted on the ground, so most of the time you know that the worst that could happen isn't that bad, it's also something where you should make a strategy and get back from where it's going to happen. And you should hopefully start listing and taking steps on a few items that can reduce the probability that this worse case situation will occur. By doing this, you gain insight into the problem, and what you can do about all this, so anxiety appears to get a little smaller.

Add hope and optimism to someone else's life

If you get caught in depressive feelings or persecution complex, then one of the best ways to get out of your mind and the thoughts bouncing about in there is to concentrate forward and on something else. By incorporating positivity into others' lives in every way, you will start to feel happier and more hopeful again. There are a few ways to bring positivity to somebody's life:

Be useful to everyone. Give a compliment, hold the door, or let others get into your lane when driving your car.

Help others. Give others a piece of helpful advice that has helped you or helped you drive home or organize and practice for the party next week.

Just be right there. Listen in a concentrated way for a few minutes as they vent. Or talk about their challenging condition and help them try to find their way out of it.

Be happy for a few things that you can always take it for granted

It's easy to miss the good stuff about life when we feel pessimistic. Especially those that are just a natural part of life that we can take for granted a little too much. Some of the things I want to reflect on and feel thankful for in such negative moments are:

- Three daily meals a day.
- Exercise regularly
- Go for a walk

Begin tomorrow in a way that creates the right tone for the day

How you start a day also lays the foundation for it. A gloomy or pessimistic start makes it impossible to turn things around. But a good beginning makes it a lot easier to keep up with the feeling and the constructive way of thinking before it's bedtime again. A few easy ways to get the day off to a good start is:

- **It's an easy notification that you see right after you wake up**

It could be one or a few quotations that motivate you. Or maybe the target or the dream you're most enthusiastic about right now. Write it down on a sheet of paper and put it on a bedside table or a refrigerator. Or type it as part of the lock screen on your touchscreen.

- **Have a constructive knowledge or dialogue that's running into your brain**

Listen to a show, read a blog page, or read a chapter of a novel that motivates you or makes you laugh. Or share a friendly or uplifting talk with your spouse, your children, or your teammate.

CHAPTER 7: WHAT IS STRESS AND HOW TO REDUCE-IT

Stress is the way human beings respond physically and psychologically to transitions, events, and circumstances in their lives. People are facing tension in different ways and for different reasons. The answer is based on your interpretation of an incident or circumstance. If you perceive the situation negatively, you are likely to feel depressed—frustrated, oppressed, or out of control. Distress is a more familiar type of stress. The other type, eustress, is the product of a "positive" view of an incident or situation, which is why it is often called "healthy tension." Eustress makes you respond to a task and can be an antidote to boredom because it engages concentrated attention. The energy will quickly transform to distress, though, if it triggers anything. You see, the situation is unsustainable or out of control. Many people consider public speaking or aerial flights to be rather tricky, triggering physical reactions such as elevated heart rate and lack of appetite, whilst others are looking forward to the experience. It's often a matter of perception: a positive stress response for one person may be a negative stressor for another.

Stress impacts us in a lot of ways, both physically and mentally, and in several ways. Research has demonstrated that anxiety can be optimistic at times. It makes us more alert and allows us to do well in some circumstances. However, stress is significant only if it is short-lived. Excessive or chronic stress can lead to diseases such as heart disease and mental health conditions, such as anxiety and depression. In circumstances that make you feel threatened or irritated, the body produces a stress reaction. This can induce several physical effects, alter the way you respond, and drive you to more extreme emotions.

Types of stress

The most frequent explanations for "stressing" fell into three major categories:

1. Unsettling consequences of the transition

2. Feeling like an outside power is questioning you or influencing you

3. The sense like you have lost control of yourself

Life occurrences such as marriage, career transitions, divorce, or the loss of a relative or an acquaintance are the most common sources of stress. Although life-threatening incidents are less frequent, they can be the most physiologically and psychologically acute. They are typically related to public service occupations in which people face high levels of tension due to potential threats and high levels of confusion among police officers, fire and rescue personnel, disaster relief workers, and the military. You may not plan to pursue a high-stress career, but as a college student, you can find that the stresses of college life may contribute to difficult circumstances. The National Institute of Mental Health (NIMH) lists some of the most critical stressors for college students:

- Increased academic standards
- To be on your own in a new setting
- Improvements in family dynamics
- Economic obligation
- The rapid change in your community interaction
- Introduction to new people, ideas, and impulses
- Awareness of your gender orientation and alignment
- Preparation for life following graduation

Signs and symptoms of distress

Stress signs fall into three general but interrelated types, physical, behavioral, and emotional. And check this collection carefully. If you find yourself feeling these symptoms regularly, you are likely to feel distressed:

- Headache
- Fatigue
- Stomach Concerns
- Hypertension (high blood pressure)
- Heart issues, such as vibration
- Failure to concentrate / lack of focus
- Sleep disruptions, whether it is sleeping too lengthy or not being able to sleep
- Sweating palms and shaky hands
- Anxiety
- Sexual disorders

Even if you don't know it, stress may cause or lead to severe physical disorders. It increases hormones such as cortisol and corticosterone that influence your metabolism, immune reactions, and other stress reactions. This will lead to a rise in your pulse rate, breathing, blood pressure, and physical pressures on your internal organs. Behavioral shifts are also stressed expressions. They may include:

- Creativity
- Disruptive food habits (overeating or under-eating)
- Terrible act for others
- Substantially increase smoking or intake of alcohol.
- Isolation
- Mandatory shopping.

A sustained high degree of tension is no laugh. It can impact any aspect of your job and educational life productivity, enhanced health risks, and relationships, to name just a few.

Physical Signs and Symptoms

People respond differently to tension. Any typical signs of stress include sleepiness, sweating, or changes in appetite. Symptoms such as this are caused by a surge of stress hormones in your body that, when released, help you to cope with stresses or risks. This is referred to as the "fight or flight" reaction. Hormones called adrenaline and noradrenaline increase your blood pressure, increase your pulse rate, and increase the rate at which you start sweating. This will ready the body for emergency response. These hormones will also reduce blood supply to the skin and reduce stomach function. Cortisol, another stress hormone, releases fat and sugar to your system to improve your performance. As a result, you might feel headache, muscle stiffness, discomfort, nausea, diarrhea, and dizziness. You can also breathe more rapidly, have headaches, or have numerous hurts and pains. In the long run, you can be at risk of heart problems and strokes. All these changes are the way your body makes it easy for you to fight or run away. Usually, after stress or danger has passed, the stress hormone levels will function normally. However, if you are continually under stress, these hormones will stay in the body, contributing to signs of stress. If you're trapped in a busy workplace or an overcrowded subway, you can't fight or run away because you can't use the chemicals that your own body produces to protect you. Over time, the build-up of these substances and the alterations they make can be detrimental to your health.

Cognitive and psychological consequences

When you are anxious, you can experience several different emotions, including fear, irritability, or low self-esteem, which could cause you to be distant, indecisive, or tearful. You can encounter phases of intense worry, rushing thoughts, or continuously run over the same things in your mind. Many people are noticing changes in their behavior. They can lose their patients more quickly, behave irrationally, or become more aggressive or physically violent. These emotions can feed on each other and cause physical effects that can make you feel much worse. For example, intense anxiety can make you feel so bad that you fear getting a severe physical disorder.

Identification of symptoms of stress

All are facing discomfort. However, as it impacts your life, fitness, and well-being, it is essential to overcome it as soon as possible. Although stress affects people differently, there are typical signs and symptoms that you should look for:

- Feelings of persistent fear or panic

- Thoughts of being distract
- Difficulty in focusing
- Mood swings or mood shifts
- Irritability or shortness of temper
- Having trouble to rest
- Depression
- Poor self-esteem
- Eating more or less than usual.
- Change of sleeping habits
- Use of alcohol, cigarettes, or illegal substances to calm
- Discomforts, particularly muscle tension
- Indigestion and constipation
- Sensations of fatigue or dizziness
- Loss of sex drive

If you have these effects for a more extended period and find like they affect your daily life or make you feel uncomfortable, you should talk to your GP. You should inquire about updates about the community programs and therapies available to you.

What induces stress

There are all types of circumstances that can trigger tension. The most widespread problems are jobs, money, and relationships with families, children, or other family members. Stress can be induced either by significant uprisings and life incidents such as divorce, bankruptcy, home relocation, and bereavement or by a sequence of small irritations such as feeling undervalued at work or fighting with a family member. There are sometimes no apparent reasons.

The response of the body to stress

Humans undergo a range of physiological and psychological changes as they are affected by environmental threats, changes, or demands. If the vulnerability has been identified and evaluated as hazardous, the person considers the appropriate coping tools. If the requirements of the situation are perceived to be greater than the available coping tools, an "alarm" or "Fight-or-Flight Response" is created. During the fight-or-flight reaction, the body prepares for action, which usually consists of either engaging or resisting the danger. The nervous system is stimulated, and hormones, including adrenaline and noradrenaline, are absorbed into the circulation. Heart and respiratory rates rise, and blood pressure increases, causing the body to rapidly pump oxygenated blood to the brain and muscles of the body. Blood is diverted from the extremities to the heart, and digestive processes are slowed down.

Muscles begin to become rigid, eyes open, and hearing becomes more intense. Sweat glands are stimulated to cool the body, and the skin is always browner or bright. Fight-or-flight reaction continues to produce several psychological mechanisms. Attention is heightened and narrowed, with particular emphasis on hazard related cues, and one's ability to listen to and focus on other activities can be diminished. Short-term memory and decision-making capabilities may also be adversely influenced by high tension, and mentally, people begin to feel nervous, "on the brink," fearful, anxious, and impatient. Pacing, fidgeting, and resisting habits are typical behavioral signs of stress-induced panic responses, and often people feel an impulse to avoid stressors or to escape circumstances. If a person can effectively handle or prevent a stressor, the body may continue to return to homeostasis. However, prolonged exposure to stress or repeated confrontations with traumatic stimuli can begin to affect the person.

Stress level is often correlated with several habits and lifestyle decisions that can have adverse health outcomes. Data suggests that people with high tension are more likely to participate in heavy alcohol intake and greater use of medications and tobacco products. Interestingly, alcohol raises the levels of adrenaline, which can prolong the sensation of tension induced by stress reactions. Stress may affect the way the body absorbs alcohol, decreasing the pleasant benefits of alcohol and increasing the desire for more alcohol. Besides, excessive alcohol use and tobacco use are primary causes of several chronic health conditions, including liver cancer, cirrhosis of the liver, lung cancer, chronic heart disease, and stroke. It is necessary to note that deficient levels of stress may often have detrimental effects. For instance, when arousal levels are too low, people usually feel boredom, poor cognitive and physical function, negative thinking, and loss of attention to detail. The Yerkes Dodson Law, established by psychologists in the early 1900s, maintains that the physiological and mental processing of organisms appears to be optimum after exhibiting mild to moderate levels of enthusiasm. Although the degree of tension and enthusiasm necessary for optimum functioning varies depending on the type of function, research over the last century has typically confirmed this idea, which has influenced the way stress and anxiety are conceptualized and handled.

Stress advantages and drawbacks

While stress is commonly considered to be something to prevent, stress is a normal physiological response that serves a protective role. To a moderate degree, stress helps alert us to possible environmental risks and encourages us to concentrate our efforts on mitigating the threat. Stress also gives us the energy needed to tackle or escape from the threat by a "punch-flight" reaction. While specific stress is helpful, excessive or extreme stress can be associated with several negative physical and psychological consequences. For example, while mild levels of stress tend to concentrate our attention, extreme stress contributes to decreased attention, concentrating, decision-making, and short-term memory. High stress can also lead to several mental problems, including hyperactivity, depression, and anxiety disorders. Indeed, many scholars believe stress to be a crucial component of the cause of psychological trauma. Chronic high stress is associated with significant health problems, including cardiovascular disease, asthma, immunodeficiency, and more frequent infections, sexual dysfunction, digestive disorders, and persistent headaches.

Relationships

Relationships are a great comfort at a time when we feel overwhelmed. However, from time to time, people close to you, whether you are a spouse, parent, infant, acquaintance, or colleague, can increase your stress levels. Things such as continuing small disputes and conflicts, broader family crises such as an affair, death, or grief are likely to affect the way you think, behave, and respond. As a consequence, this can affect your stress levels.

Balance in work-life

The strain of an extremely stressful work community in the United Kingdom is one of the main contributors to depression among the general population. The human cost of unmanaged work-related tension is substantial. Feeling depressed with the amount of time you spend at work and ignoring other aspects of life because of work will increase your susceptibility to stress. Increased levels of stress can, if not tackled early enough, lead to burn-out or more serious mental health issues. Mental health problems such as depression are known to be the primary cause of loss of employment, responsible for up to 40% of sick leave. Mental well-being accounted for 442,000 cases of occupational disease in 2008, at an approximate expense of £13.5 million. As a result, mental disease now accounts for a large proportion of long-term illness and early retirement, which is perceived to be the primary cause of illness for 20 percent of the national health care staff.

Financial issues

Money and debt issues put enormous pressure on us, so it doesn't come as a surprise that they have a significant impact on our stress levels. In any capacity, the consequences of the global downturn have impacted everybody. The latest figures from organizational culture Debt Charity revealed a 56% growth in demand for debt advice and assistance from 2012-2014. Citizens Advice has seen a similar rise in the number of individuals facing financial hardship, coping with 6,407 debt issues per working day. A study published in 2013 revealed that 42% of those pursuing financial assistance had been given medications by their GP to help them cope, while 76% of those in a couple said debt had impaired their relationship. The mixture of constant stress and debt will lead to depression and anxiety and has been highlighted as a cause linked to suicidal thoughts and attempts. It's crucial if you're concerned about your finances and debts that you're not struggling to deal with them on your own.

Smoking, drinking, and drugs abuse

Some people smoke, consume alcohol, and use recreation medications to relieve tension. However, this also allows things to get worse. Research suggests that smoking can raise feelings of anxiety. Nicotine produces an acute, transient feeling of relief, which can lead to withdrawal effects and cravings. Similarly, people may use alcohol as a way of controlling and dealing with complicated feelings and temporarily reducing feelings of anxiety. However, this is alcohol will make current mental health conditions worse. In the long term, it will make you feel more nervous and sadder. It is necessary to know the prescribed limits and to drink responsibly. Prescription medications, such as tranquilizers and sleeping pills, which may have been administered for particular purposes, may also cause emotional and physical health issues if they are taken for extended periods. Street drugs, such as cocaine or ecstasy, are commonly used for recreational activities. For some of the Users, complications begin when their bodies get used to the repeated use of medications. This contributes to the need for elevated doses to preserve the same effect.

How can you help yourself with that?

Stress is a natural solution to stressful circumstances in life, such as jobs, families, relationships, and money issues. We discussed earlier that a mild level of stress could make us work better in stressful conditions, but overstress or prolonged stress can contribute to physical issues. This can involve reduced immune levels, digestive and intestinal difficulties such as irritable bowel syndrome (IBS), or mental health issues such as depression. It is also crucial that we control our stress and keep it at a safe level to avoid long-term harm to our bodies and minds. When you feel stressed out, consider taking these.

Steps:

- Know that you have a problem with it. You ought to make a correlation between feeling exhausted or sick and the stresses you're under. Do not disregard physical signs such as tense muscles, exhaustion, headaches, or insomnia.

- Recognize the causes of this. Please strive to establish the root factors. Filter the potential explanations for your tension into those with a realistic answer, those that would be easier given time regardless, and those you can't do anything. Learn to let go of those in the second and third classes – there's no use in thinking about stuff you can't fix or things you're going to figure out.

- Check out your lifestyle. Are you taking so much of that? Is there stuff you're doing that should be turned off to anyone else? Will you do it more comfortably? You might need to plan stuff that you're trying to do and reorganize your life so that you don't have to do it all at once.

It can also help to shield you from tension in a variety of ways:

- **Eat a healthy diet.** A healthy and balanced diet can minimize the risk of diet-related illnesses. There is now a growing amount of research demonstrating how food influences our mood. Feelings of well-being will be preserved by ensuring that our diet contains sufficient levels of brain foods, such as essential vitamins and minerals, as well as water.

You ought to be mindful of smoking and alcohol. And if it can appear to relieve anxiety, this is deceptive since they also make things worse.

- **Do workout regularly.** Physical exercise can be beneficial in alleviating stress. And getting out getting some fresh air and some light physical activity, including walking to the stores, will help.

Take some time out of routine. Take the time to rest. Saying 'I really can't take time off' is not a smart option if you are pressured to take time off later due to ill health. Finding a balance between responsibility towards others and responsibility towards oneself is key to lowering stress levels.

- **Mindfulness.** Mindfulness meditation should be performed at any moment. Research has shown that it can alleviate the symptoms of stress, anxiety, and other associated issues, such as insomnia, weak concentration, and depressed moods, in some individuals.

- **Take peaceful sleep.** Sleeping issues are typical when you're under stress. Try to make sure you have ample rest.

- **Don't be too harsh on yourself.** Just remember to put things in perspective. We all have bad days, after all.

Looking for support

It's all right to ask for additional support if you like you're unable to cope on your own. It's essential to find treatment as quickly as possible so that you can start to get better. Your family doctor is the first one to approach you. He or she may be able to provide recommendations on care and be able to refer you to another local specialist. Cognitive Behavioral Therapy and Mindfulness-based techniques are considered to help relieve stress. Several charitable programs will help you discuss the sources of depression and offer guidance on how to feel healthier.

Management of stress

Despite the positive nature of mild to moderate degrees of stress, the purpose of stress control is not to remove any stress. Instead, tension control strategies are designed to keep stress levels within the optimum range. Engaging in a balanced lifestyle will help alleviate depression and increase the possibility of a long, healthy life. Empirical evidence has strongly endorsed the following stress control techniques: physical activity and exercise; balanced eating; adequate sleep; healing, meditation and mindfulness; humor, self-expression, and social support; and behavior modification.

Vigorous exercise and training

Considerable research has accrued that routine physical activity is associated with a variety of physical and psychological health effects. For example, frequent participation in mild exercises, such as fast walking, improves the immune system and lowers disease rates. Exercise also improves the muscles of the body, especially the heart, maintains muscle fat, and assists in weight loss. Individuals who exercise consistently are often at a lower risk for some chronic conditions, such as diabetes and hypertension. While exercise is technically a stressor itself, forcing the body to respond to the demands of the workout, research shows that daily physical exercise can help to minimize the body's reaction to other stressors. In particular, several studies have found that individuals who exercise display lower physiological (e.g., blood pressure, heart rate) signs of stress and experience less discomfort in response to a problematic condition than people who do not exercise. This observation is especially significant considering that stressful experiences precede nearly 80% of major depressive episodes, and stress is a basic risk factor for the occurrence of panic attacks, widespread anxiety, posttraumatic stress, social anxiety, and mental illnesses. As a consequence, participation in physical exercise may help to defend against or avoid the onset of anxiety and mood disruptions.

Besides, the accumulation of evidence shows that routine physical exercise is beneficial in addressing many of these disorders as they arise. Some studies say that exercise is as successful as psychotherapy or medical care of some anxiety and mood disturbances. For example, in one study, individuals who suffered repeated panic attacks responded to 12 weeks of aerobic exercise like those on clinical drugs. Another study has shown that aerobic activity decreases the severity of symptoms in people with obsessive-compulsive disorder, and a recent study of 11 trials comparing the impact of daily exercise with depression psychotherapy has found that two to four workout sessions per week are just as effective in managing depression as psychotherapy. Furthermore, while most clinicians suggest daily participation in fitness regimens to optimize benefits, evidence shows that even single weightlifting will minimize perceived stress levels and boost mood. It seems like the workout is a treatment.

Healthy diet

Research shows that many people change their eating habits when they encounter elevated levels of stress. One of the most frequent stress-related dietary changes includes increased intake of caffeine in an attempt to boost early morning or late-night efficiency. Ironically, while caffeine is associated with a short-term improvement in alertness, caffeine can also intensify the stress reaction. For example, caffeine activates the body to release various stress hormones, including Serotonin and glucocorticoids, as well as monoamine neurotransmitters, including dopamine and adrenaline. The release of these chemicals is related to elevated levels of stress for hours after ingestion. Also, caffeine intake can contribute to other disorders that may impair your body's ability to react to stress, like insomnia, depression, increased risk of cardiac disease, gastrointestinal problems, and immune system suppression, making you more susceptible to infection. As noted earlier, elevated levels of stress are often associated with rises in cortisol, which appear to contribute to high-fat or sugary food cravings. Also, when active, people sometimes have to miss meals or eat fast food. These dietary modifications will make it increasingly challenging for our bodies to manage stress.

Eating a balanced diet full of nutrient-rich foods will help you survive depression in a variety of ways. For instance, complex carbohydrates, such as oatmeal and whole-grain pieces of bread and cereals, allow the brain to release Serotonin, a neurotransmitter correlated with an optimistic attitude. Also, essential carbohydrates, such as sugar or chocolate, can be useful for a fast boost in Serotonin.

Data shows that foods high in vitamin C (e.g., oranges) and omega-3 fatty acids (e.g., salmon) can help lower stress hormone levels and enhance immune function. A well-balanced diet increases one's ability to handle stress.

Appropriate sleep

Data shows that the association between stress and sleep is bidirectional in that elevated levels of stress appear to be correlated with impaired sleep, and lack of sleep appears to intensify stress. Numerous studies have found that chronic stress appears to suppress sleep and rest, increase the rate of nightmares, and decrease the quality of sleep. Numerous stress-and anxiety-related emotional disorders, such as posttraumatic stress disorder and generalized anxiety disorder, are also associated with severe sleep disturbance.

On the other hand, lack of adequate sleep also contributes to under-optimal physiological and psychological functioning. For example, sleepless individuals experience higher levels of stress, anxiety, and frustration in response to even low-level physiological stress. Besides, some research shows that sleep deficiency influences the levels of cortisol (a stress hormone) and neuroimaging findings demonstrate that sleep deprivation is correlated with compromised neurological functions, including enhanced amygdala (part of the brain associated with emotional reactions) reactivity and pre-frontal brain regulation. Also, there is ample evidence that poor sleep is associated with low immune functioning. Epidemiological evidence shows that most people need 7 to 8 hours of sleep every night to get the full physiological and psychological benefits from sleep.

Relief, relaxation, mindfulness

Contentment or relaxation of physical or emotional stress is also considered to be an antidote to stress. Relaxation and anxiety are considered to be antagonistic to feelings so that one cannot be calm and nervous at the same time. In reality, maintaining a state of relaxation during a time of stress is always a challenging activity. However, several methods have been devised to help us achieve a state of equilibrium, some of which have proven reliable effectiveness in psychological research: neuromuscular breathing, gradual muscle relaxation, guided imaging, and mediation practices. Deep abdominal breathing is a procedure intended to slow down one's breathing and control the absorption of oxygen. Diaphragmatic breathing requires slow, deep breathing to extend and contract the diaphragm, a muscle that divides the chest and abdominal cavities. Usually, diaphragmatic breathing techniques include sitting in a relaxed chair or lying down and breathing gently, comfortably, to breathe so that the air expands the belly more than the lung.

Research shows that diaphragmatic breathing will dramatically minimize perceived stress. A group of medical school students engaged in a deep breathing regimen for 5 minutes per day before class over ten months in one study. After six weeks, students participating in deep breathing exercises showed substantially less test anxiety, self-doubt, lack of confidence, and increased focus during tests. Progressive musical series of progressive muscle relaxation procedures involving repeated stress and relaxation of different muscle groups in the body. Deep breathing is also combined, and the person undergoes deep breathing exercises while also tensioning and calming muscle groups. PMR aims to affect the inhibitory arousal portion of stress and anxiety by reducing skeletal muscle tension. Other forms of autonomic excitement, such as blood, are thought to decline as skeletal muscle stress decreases. While the initial progressive muscle relaxation paradigm was highly time-consuming (i.e., requiring almost 30 muscle groups and up to 100 individual practice sessions over months or years), subsequent studies indicated that similar results could be achieved with far fewer sessions. Similar to breathing techniques, PMR sessions typically entail taking a relaxed posture and deep breathing while tensioning and calming 16 different muscle groups (e.g., beginning with the muscles of the head and progressing down the body until stopping with the legs). As part of the

Personal Discovery Appraisal (PDA) in this module, you will have the chance to experience PMR directly.

Guided imagery, or simulation, refers to a form of stimulation preparation that includes the use of words to construct a relaxing, sensory environment rich in one's imagination. While guided imaging strategies can vary greatly, most include directing individuals to areas or contexts in which they feel relaxed and secure and empowering individuals free their minds from any intrusion or everyday concerns. For instance, a session could be to make a person pretend that they're sitting on a peaceful beach on a perfect beach weather day or in the woods next to a gentle stream. Research shows that guided imaging strategies are successful in minimizing stress and raising healthy moods. Guided visualization has also been found to improve feelings of well-being and peacefulness in people with a broad spectrum of chronic diseases. Similar to diaphragmatic breathing, meditation techniques incorporate concentrating on a single object or sensation (such as breathing) while disconnecting from all distractors and controlling internal sensations (i.e., feelings, thoughts) through non-judgmental acceptance. Study shows that meditation is adversely associated with perceived stress and reduces Cortisol serum (stress hormone) levels. Besides, meditation is positively correlated with several calming markers, such as lowered skeletal muscle metabolism, enhanced heart rate, and increased alpha wave activity. It is correlated with increased sociability, empathic, and optimistic thought. In general, several relaxing techniques have been found to relieve stress and enhance mental well-being. If it's diaphragmatic breathing, PMR, directed visualization, meditation, or a host of others not mentioned here, it only takes a few minutes to increase stress levels.

Laughing, self-assertiveness, and social support

It has long been said that "laughing is the greatest cure." Yes, we now know that laughter causes many beneficial biochemical and psychological improvements in the body. Analysis reveals that laughing raises oxygen consumption and activates various muscles and organs, including the heart and lungs. Laughter also decreases blood pressure and blood sugar levels, increases blood supply, and boosts energy levels. Also, laughing triggers the production of endorphins, which can improve the resistance of pain and produce euphoria.

Humor offers a social break from the present situation, which helps us to substitute our pessimistic assessments with more constructive ones. Some evidence shows that laughter can be as beneficial as mild aerobic exercise or relaxation therapy to boost mood. Suppressing negative emotions will increase tension and, in turn, harm one's health. The study, however, shows that the development of negative feelings in an adaptive and socially appropriate way will minimize stress and enhance immune function. For example, one study showed that a group of international students who wrote about their most traumatic or painful encounters for 20 minutes per day over three days reported substantially minimum stress than their peers who wrote about the positive experience. The physical and psychological benefits of transparency are not restricted to literature. Talking about profoundly upsetting or stressful events has been proven to alleviate fear, fatigue, and dysphonia. One of the most common ways of therapeutic therapy for stress problems includes consciously remembering and regularly communicating about stressful experiences until the incident is less disturbing.

A healthy social support structure is also useful in dealing with pressures. Evidence shows that the strength of one's social support network is an indicator of well-being and is adversely correlated with many mental health circumstances. On the other hand, depression is associated with a variety of health conditions, including elevated blood pressure, and depressed people have more negative encounters and are more likely to assess circumstances as stressful. Researchers suggest that higher levels of perceived tension may explain the poorer health outcomes of lonely people. They also found that depression mediates the relationship between social support and well-being. Loneliness is better protected against the consistency or closeness of relationships over quantity or amount of relationships. Efforts should then be made in concrete partnerships rather than innumerable peripheral ones.

Behavioral structuring

Sometimes, we presume that the events we witness have a substantial impact on our feelings. For instance, finding out that you did a lousy exam score or that your girlfriend wants to break up with you causes people to feel depressed. It is not, though, the incident itself that contributes to emotion. Instead, it is the sign that you provide to the incident or the perception of the situation that defines the emotional effect of the event. If you take the terrible grade to mean that you're not smart or that you're never going to surpass in school, no matter how hard you try, you're likely to feel a depressive mood. On the other hand, whether you view the grade as a fluke or a wake-up call you wanted to improve your enthusiasm for learning, the attitude is likely to be much less pessimistic.

As you can see, the way we view or learn of a circumstance or occurrence can have a dramatic effect on the emotions we feel. The cognitive restructuring includes learning to recognize irrational or ill-adapted feelings that we encounter that lead to depressive moods and then modifying them to represent the situation more correctly. E.g., whether you're planning for a presentation, and you always think, "I know I'm going to say something foolish, and everybody's going to laugh at me" or, "Everybody's going to be able to see how stressed I am, and they're going to think I'm an asshole," you're likely to be quite anxious. But are these honest thoughts? Unless you are especially adept at forecasting the future (in which case, I would love some guidance in choosing my lottery numbers!), these thoughts are typically indicators of disastrous thoughts that raise anxiety.

Although you could suggest something dumb, what are the chances if you plan and rehear the presentation thoroughly? How many times did you give a presentation in the past and don't mention something stupid? And if you say anything that doesn't sound exceptionally intelligent, is it likely that any, most, or all of the students in the class would not hear or think badly about you? If people note your anxiety, is it likely that they will view it in a better manner than thinking that you're an idiot? "Can any people have no sympathy for you, given that public speaking is one of the biggest concerns among college students? After criticizing irrational or ill-adapted reasoning in this way, it is important to choose a rational alternative to replace it. A more reasonable alternative to the first assertion might be, "If I plan properly and know what I'm going to say in advance, I'll probably do a decent job of explaining the presentation." For the second argument, you might substitute, "most people will be nervous before they present, and even if they note my discomfort, they'll probably be able to relate to it."

The stress relief medication

To increase your capacity to cope with stress, consider the following:

- **Exercise daily.** Engage in 3-5 sessions of low-intensity workout a week to improve your immune system and reduce your chances of anxiety and mood disorders. However, even though you can't work out daily, note that even a single episode of workout can be a perfect way to alleviate tension and improve your mood.

- **Have a balanced meal.** Eat lots of fruit, salads, whole grains, and fatty fish to maximize your physical well-being and your body's capacity to relieve stress.

- **Sleep.** Take 7-8 hours of continuous sleep a night to increase your mood and boost your immune system.

- **Learn to relax.** Engage in calming activities daily or during times of mild to extreme tension. Progressive muscle relaxation (PMR), guided imaging, and meditation are excellent ways to reduce the overall level of enthusiasm. Or incorporate exercise with meditation or mindfulness by investing in yoga two or three days a week.

- **Express yourself.** Look for the humor in difficult times, and find ways to communicate the feelings by poetry, painting, or talking to friends and family.
- **Contextualize.** Take note of how you learn about and view difficult circumstances and search for reasons to reframe the situation more reasonably or constructively.

Depression

Unfortunately, the inability of a person to cope with stress will also lead to acute depression. People with depression have symptoms similar to stress, except that the symptoms are not temporary; they can last for weeks or even months. The impacts on the body, mood, and behavior are much more severe than temporary stress due to continuous symptoms. Depression will have significant diseaimpacts on your eating habits, your relationships, your ability to work and learn, and how you think and feel. The condition is not specific to a single group of persons or areas of the world. Millions of adults, including many college students, are suffering from psychiatric depression. It is important to remember that psychiatric depression is a real condition, not an "imaginary" one. This is not a changing mood or a sign of emotional vulnerability. It needs treatment, and 80 percent of those treated continue to feel better after just a few weeks. The signs and symptoms, according to NIMH, are signs of severe depression:

- Depression, fear, or "empty" feelings
- Reduced capacity, exhaustion, being slowed down
- Lack of interest or enjoyment in daily tasks
- Sleep disorders (insomnia, oversleep, or wake up even earlier than usual)
- Appetite and weight changes (loss or gain)
- Thoughts of hopelessness, remorse, and worthlessness
- Fears of death or suicide, or attempted suicide
- Difficulty in thinking, making decisions or recalling.
- Irritability or unnecessary crying
- Persistent aches and pains not explained by any other physical state

It's familiar many of the time to have some symptoms of depression. But NIMH suggests that whether anyone has five or more symptoms for two weeks or longer or has significant differences in daily functioning, he or she can go to a mental health provider for assessment. Depressed people sometimes do not speak correctly, so they do not get treatment on their own. They also need support from those who "need help to get help." Mental health experts agree depression in college students is a significant concern. A recent study of first-year college students reveals that students today feel more distracted and depressed than students did 15 years earlier. The National Mental Health Association demonstrates that more than 30% of high schoolers experience feeling depressed a lot of the time. If you believe you may be stressed, you should speak to a trained health care provider or mental health professional. A resident advisor in your dormitory, a student wellness center, a family health care provider or a church member can help lead you to recovery options. Several appropriate medications for depression are available, and relief can be given after only a few weeks, depending on the severity of the symptoms. Individuals, however, respond differently to medication. If you don't get any better in a couple of weeks, speak to the care provider about other options.

Suicidal attempt

As noted before, extreme depression frequently manifests itself in thoughts of death or suicide, or suicide attempts. Many people are naturally uncomfortable talking about suicide, but doing so might save their lives. The NIMH estimates that in 2000, suicide was the eleventh leading cause of death for those aged 15 to 24. Although women are three times more likely to attempt suicide as men, men are four times as likely to succeed as women. There are several prevalent suicide myths:

- No one will save the person if someone wishes to die. Many people who dream of suicide don't want to die: they want to support it.
- If I ask anyone about suicide, I'm going to give the person the idea. Wrong. You can give comfort to the individual if you care enough to ask.
- Suicide is coming out of the blue. Wrong. Typically, the individual shows a variety of warning signs.

You should take suicidal thoughts, urges, or actions earnestly. If you hear or talk of hurting or harming yourself or know someone who is, get assistance immediately. The NIMH advises that you turn to your health center; a family physician, a professor, mentor, or adviser; a church member; a nearby suicide or ambulance hotline; or a hospital emergency department.

Some early signs of suicide involve:

- To talk about suicide.
- Declarations of hopelessness, helplessness, or powerlessness
- Anxiety over mortality
- Feeling unexpectedly happy or calmer.
- Losing confidence in items that one cares about
- Putting one's affairs for no particular cause, such as giving away precious assets or making definitive agreements concerning finances and land

100 approaches to alleviate stress: making the balancing Act more achievable

About 70 and 80 percent of all disorders and illnesses are related to stress and pressure. Chronic diseases are the primary causes of death. Yet we don't need figures to remind us that we feel depressed, tired, and creatively exhausted because we don't think for ourselves. Here is a list of 100 methods of mitigating stress.

Environmental regulations

The first domain to look for how to minimize tension is the environment surrounding you. What do you see, sense, hear, touch, taste? What's going to make you lower your shoulders and think, "Ah ... Seek opportunities to bring elegance to the surroundings. Here are a couple of things to get you begun:

1.   Enjoy being together

2.   Light a fragrant candle

3.   Please try hypnotherapy

4.   Bake the bread or biscuits

5.   Switch the illumination

6.   Grow plants

7.   Buy a bouquet of your own

8.   Build a list of items that you enjoy

9.   Put on a bird feeder and monitor it.

10.   Could you read it in the sunlight?

11.   Sip a hot drink or an iced drink

12.   Cuddle under a blanket with a book

Creative methods

Creativity is a perfect way to bring stress to fashion. Using the arts to relax and evaluate all the challenges at the same time. The result is not as important as the process itself. There are a few innovative methods for alleviating stress:

1. Write Journal
2. Write a note to you
3. Do painting
4. Drawing
5. Spend a shooting day.
6. Develop pottery/clay work
7. Knit, Sew, Needlework
8. Stroke your cat
9. Listen to pleasant songs
10. Play an instrument
11. Take part in a concert
12. Begin your better routine
13. Garden the Plant

Psychological methods

The second area you need to explore when mitigating tension is how you learn about and interpret knowledge. Mental interpretations will decide your emotional response, but focusing on challenges, dreaming about worst-case situations, and betting on errors will all raise your stress levels. Alternatively, encourage yourself to make errors, step on the dream of the possible outcomes, and view mistakes as the development opportunities required will reduce the stress load. Here are other emotional stress-reduction strategies:

1. Contextualize the issue
2. Choose optimistic thinking
3. Meditation of meaningful terms
4. Practice optimistic assertions
5. Take some responsibility for your reasoning.
6. Get a rational expectation.
7. Visualize the result you expect
8. Postpositive thinking to a mirror
9. Work on a riddle/game

Physical plan

You can also experience tension in your body by muscle spasms, nervous action, and stiffness. Shift the body by stretching, aerobic exercise or rhythmic activity to relieve pressure. Care for the body by making good dietary choices. Strive to reduce stress physically as follows:

1.   Dancing
2.   Cyclists
3.   Run
4.   Take a walk/walk in nature.
5.   Run the dog
6.   Train for a hike/marathon race
7.   Swimming
8.   Snorkeling
9.   Get a treatment
10.   Please give yourself a foot massage.
11.   Dip your feet in warm water
12.   Enjoy the steaming bubble bath.
13.   Take a yoga lesson.

14. Practicing tai chi.

15. Do incremental muscle relaxing.

16. Practice deep breathing regularly.

17. Check out the video exercise.

18. Choose a balanced diet.

19. Drink filtered water

20. Take multi-vitamin regularly

Humoristic approach

A phrase that we've got across our house is that, in some cases, you have to laugh or to weep, and we want to laugh. The laughing releases the stress. Have you ever asked, "I wanted a good laugh at you?" Do something fun to get rid of severe stress:

1. Watch a funny movie.

2. Watch a funny little comedy.

3. Read the comics book.

4. Laughing uncontrollably

5. Start sharing a new joke with a friend.

6.   Giggle with your spouse

Spiritual approach

We are holistic creatures, and the metaphysical aspect of us will help alleviate tension. Try these spiritual techniques as a therapeutic indicator of stress:

1.   Pray
2.   Meditate
3.   Practice to say thanks
4.   Participate in the service of religion
5.   Sing pleasant songs / religious songs
6.   Seek to represent other people

Management approaches

Many stresses are generated or intensified due to negative thinking, disorganization, and lack of attention to detail. By controlling time, money, schedules, and clumsiness, you can make a difference in how you feel in as little as 15 minutes. These management techniques are as follows:

1. Manage the time
2. Prioritizing duties
3. Distribute
4. Set a plan and follow it
5. Problem solves a dilemma
6. clean up a room
7. Organize the closet/cabinet
8. Set the priorities
9. Record of life list
10. Use the conceptual picture of success

Relational approaches

As long as we connect with people, we're going to have a friendship tension. It's also more essential in the friendship that is significant to us. Although partnerships can cause anxiety, they are also a source of stress relief. Try these relational techniques to alleviate stress:

1. Cook a special dinner for your loved one
2. Please be assertive
3. Vent to your mate
4. Meet someone to have dinner/coffee
5. Calling your mate
6. Get your manicure
7. Get your haircut, and enjoy the shower.
8. Email to an old friend
9. Enter the Mutual Support Network
10. Start the fitness class/group
11. Forgive the Injury
12. Volunteer
13. Just do anything for fun.

Outdoor plan

We started with environmental policies, and we're looking to finish with outdoor strategies. Being outdoors will change our mood, very only, by giving us a different outlook. No matter the climate or temperature, you can incorporate outdoor techniques for a fast or straightforward stress reliever. Some outdoor techniques that may be useful are as follows:

1. Lie on the bench of the park and use the sensations
2. Walk around the zoo or the aquarium.
3. Star Gazing
4. Spend a little time boating/sailing
5. Take your scenic trip
6. Build a castle of sand
7. Build up a snowman
8. Listen to the clatter of a fire in the tent.
9. Picnic next to the river
10. Go out for dinner
11. Window shopping

CONCLUSION

The researchers integrated all the findings and concluded that therapeutic communication is the purposeful interpersonal information transmitting process through words and behaviors based on client and therapist's knowledge, attitudes, and skills, which leads to patient understanding and participation. Therapeutic communication, which is intended to help the patient, involves the interpersonal communication between the patient and the nurse. Therapeutic communication techniques infer independence on the patient. The role of the healthcare professional is then to use this information to help the client further investigate his own feelings and options. Therapeutic communication requires awareness of the professional towards what is being said as well as any nonverbal cues. The mental health professional must pay special attention to the patient and the techniques followed as s/he might unconsciously influence the patient through the use of non-therapeutic techniques. The role of the health care professional in determining the illness through the steps and techniques followed is the key to successful therapeutic communication. Therapeutic communication is a purposeful form of communication, allowing the health professional and the patient to reach health-related goals through participation in a focused relationship. Barriers to communication may have a negative effect on the patient, lowering the patient's self-esteem, and may block communication. Collaboration with all the members of the health care team might be considered the key to successful therapeutic communication.

COPYRIGHT

This book:

"Acceptance and Commitment Therapy: Realm your life, reduces the stress, and manages your thoughts with the best strategies (Act prep guide)."

Written By

Alexander Harris

This document aims to provide precise and reliable details on this subject and the problem under discussion.

A legal or qualified guide is required. A person must have the right to participate in the field.

A statement of principle is a subcommittee of the American Bar Association, a committee of publishers, and is approved. A copy, reproduction, or distribution of parts of this text, in electronic or written form, is not permitted.

The recording of this document is strictly prohibited. Any retention of this text is only with the written permission of the publisher and all liberties authorized.

The information provided here is correct and reliable, as any lack of attention or other means resulting from the misuse or use of the procedures or instructions contained therein is the total and absolute obligation of the user addressed.

The author is not obliged, directly or indirectly, to assume civil liability for any restoration, damage, or loss resulting from the data collected here. The respective authors retain all copyrights not kept by the publisher.

The information contained herein is solely and universally available for information purposes. The data is presented without a warranty or promise of any kind.

The trademarks used are without approval, and the patent is issued without the trademark owner's permission or protection.

The logos and labels in this book are the property of the owners themselves and are not associated with this text.

Made in the USA
Coppell, TX
28 November 2020

42368026R00193